ACCESSORY BLDG (REF. SHT. A5.04)
Living Room
Casual Dining
ALIGN
18" ABV.
4'-7 1/4"

C.3D
3'-10"
C.8
15'-10 1/4"
20'-11 1/2"
15'-2 3/4"
EQ.

TRAMONTO RESIDENCE

ShubinDonaldson

PHOTOGRAPHY BY FERNANDO GUERRA & ROGER DAVIES

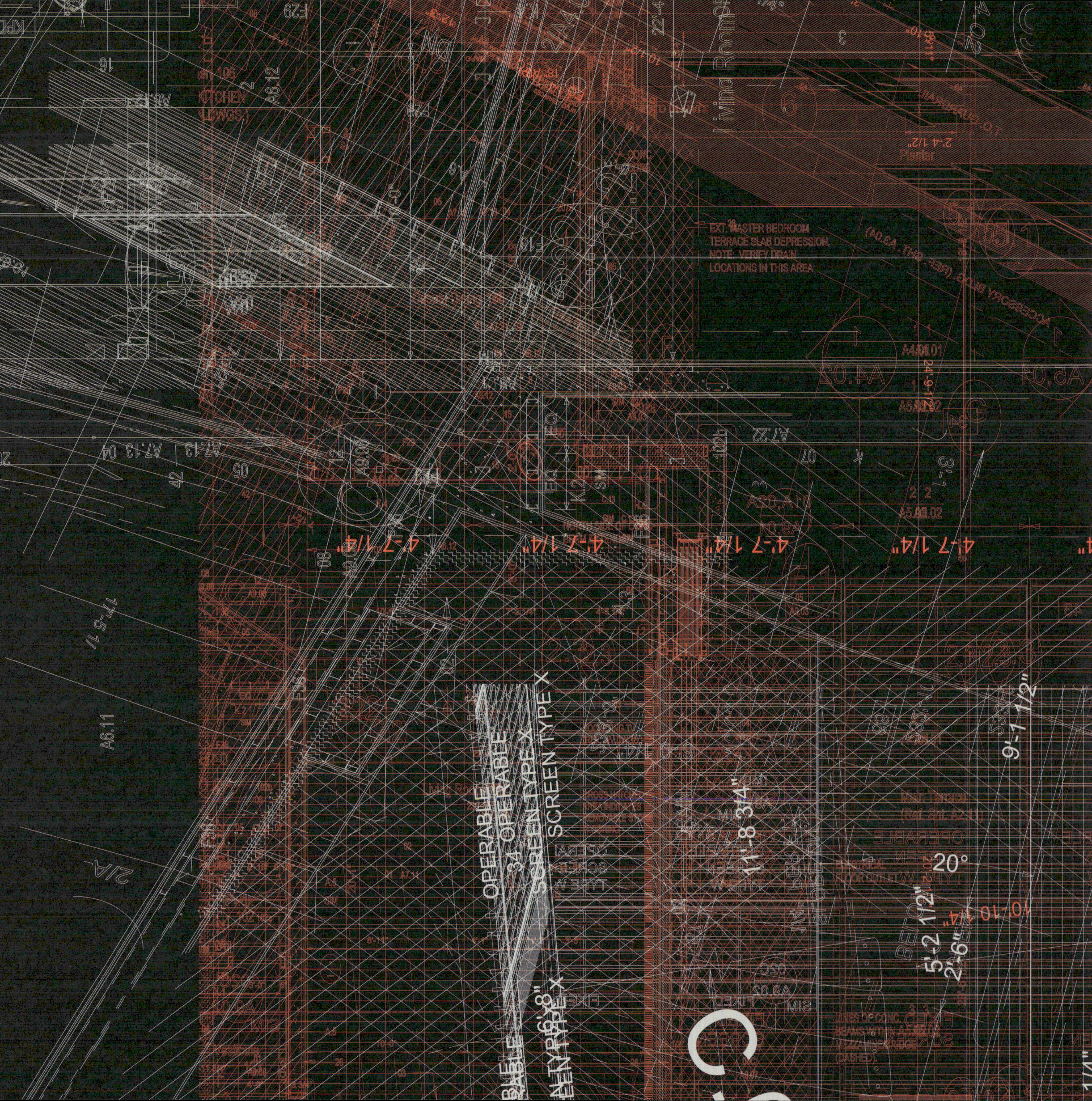

ORO EDITIONS
Publishers of Architecture, Art, and Design
Gordon Goff: Publisher

www.oroeditions.com
info@oroeditions.com

Published by ORO Editions

Graphic Design: Robin Donaldson, AIA
Text: ShubinDonaldson
Copy Edits: Julia Van Den Hout | Original Copy
ORO Project Coordinator: Kirby Anderson

10 9 8 7 6 5 4 3 2 1 First Edition

Library of Congress data available upon request. World Rights: Available

ISBN: 978-1-943532-99-5

Color Separations and Printing: ORO Group Ltd.
Printed in China.

International Distribution: www.oroeditions.com/distribution

ORO Editions makes a continuous effort to minimize the overall carbon footprint of its publications. As part of this goal, ORO Editions, in association with Global ReLeaf, arranges to plant trees to replace those used in the manufacturing of the paper produced for its books. Global ReLeaf is an international campaign run by American Forests, one of the world's oldest nonprofit conservation organizations. Global ReLeaf is American Forests' education and action program that helps individuals, organizations, agencies, and corporations improve the local and global environment by planting and caring for trees.

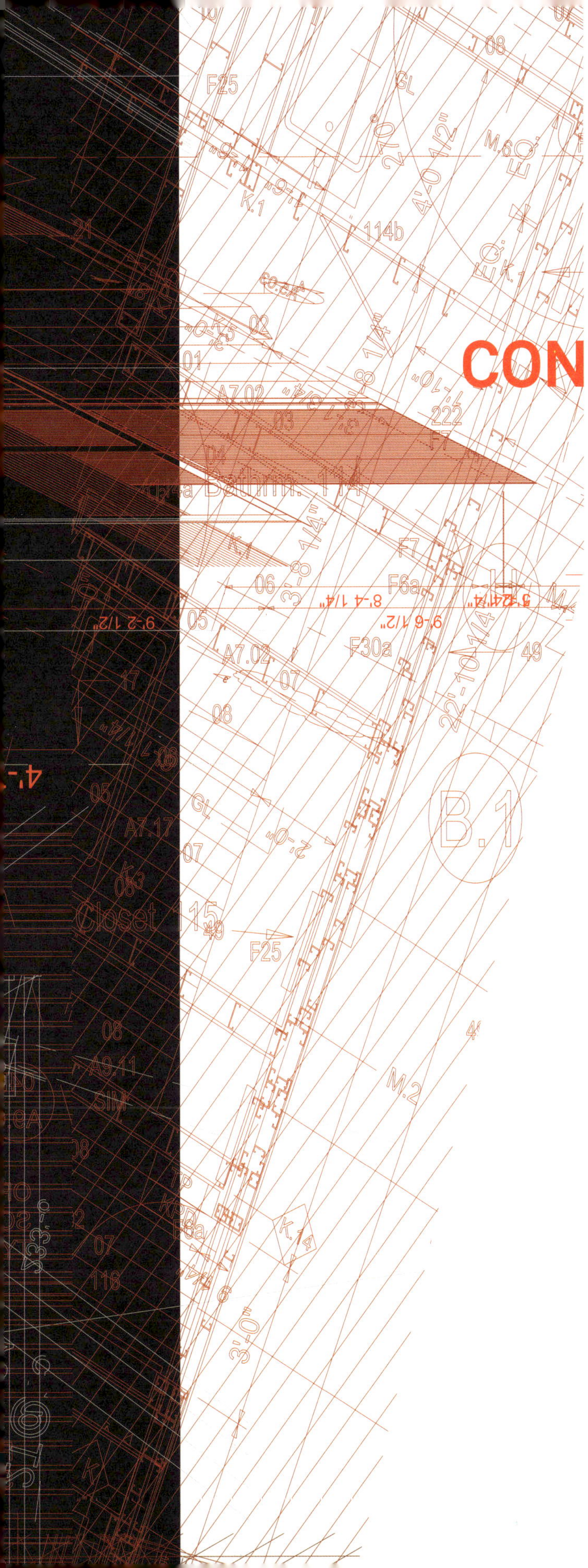

CONTENTS

EMERGENCE

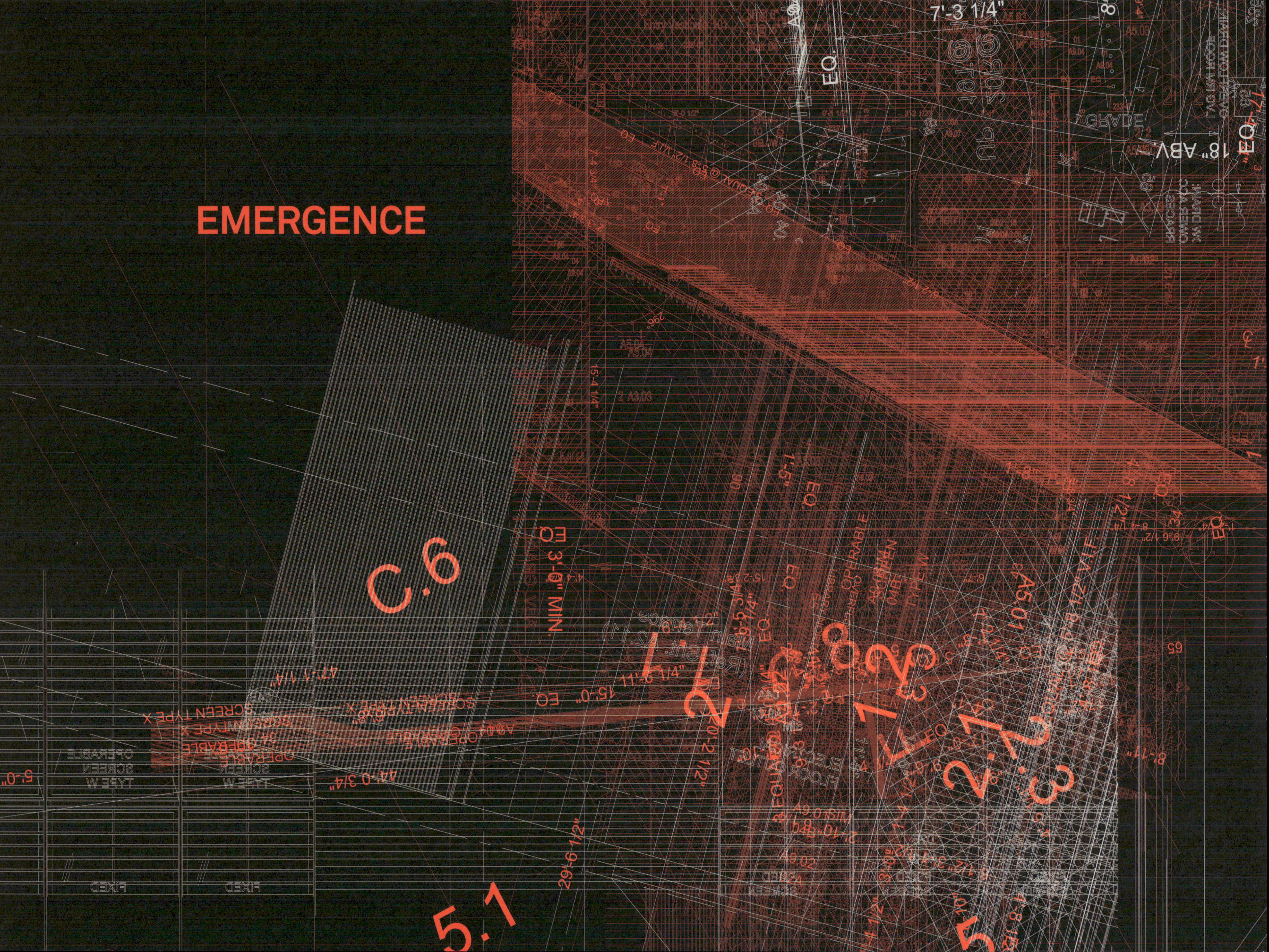

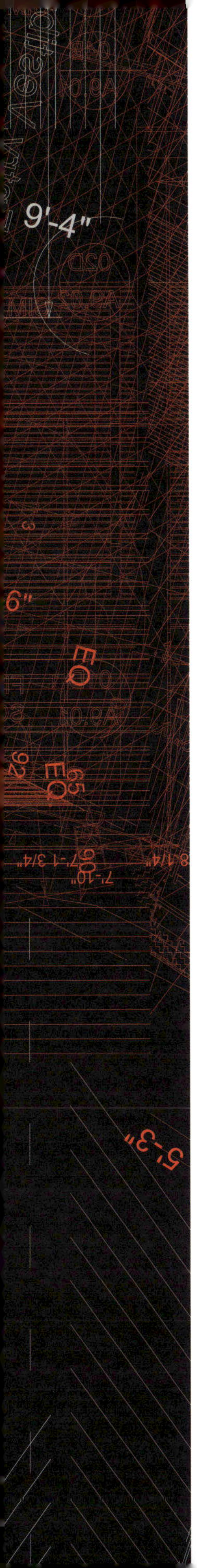

Nestled in the foothills of the Pacific Palisades, the Tramonto Residence is a contemporary single-family home integrated with the surrounding natural beauty. The house overlooks the Los Liones Canyon and Topanga State Park, the Santa Monica Mountains, and the California coastline meeting the Pacific Ocean. The 14,500 square foot (1350 m2) house blends into the natural contours of the hillside, ascending the steep topography with terraced levels while maintaining a subtle overall profile and reinforcing the slope with its sub-grade structure.

Central to the design of the residence is its strong connection with the horizon, extending from the inside to the outside, with expansive views of coastal California. Three principle axes organize the building's design—the first addresses the ocean, the second, justified to the adjacent property line, follows the wrapping curvature of the site, and the third orients the house to the nearby canyon and foothills.

The landscape has been designed to encourage indigenous wildlife by incorporating a grove of 200 new trees and drought-tolerant planting complementing the native flora. A terraced orchard blurs the boundary between architecture and nature on the eastern edge of the residence.

The residence is approached by a dramatic climb skirting the western edge of the property. Water cascades down a stepped runnel, guiding visitors on foot from an oval entry clearing up to the residence, gradually revealing itself beyond planted terraces.

The structure is, at once, geometric and organic, horizontal and vertical, ethereal and rooted. Sharp lines are softened by a natural material palette of bright limestone, rich ipe wood, and lush plantings. The limestone facade emerges from the rocky slope and slowly dissolves into the descending terraced landscape—like a large stone artifact exposed by gradual erosion.

The entrance to the house is distinguished by the long vertical lines of the two-story-tall operable ipe wood louvers, accentuating the wide stone steps leading up to the house. The residence's interior is a spatial extension of the stepped landscape, progressing from the outdoor terrace through full-height pocket doors into the living room.

Inside, multiple site axes converge, creating harmony between subtle transitions and dynamic spatial sequences. The entrance foyer opens into a double-height living room, looking back toward the ocean. The volume shifts to the east through the main living space, encouraging further progression into the more intimate spaces of daily life. The dining room and kitchen focus on the terraced orchard, while the family room and guest suite with its disappearing corner orients toward the top of the hill.

At the center of the first level, the garage is set firmly into the hillside, affording an experience of the house's sectional nature. The garage interior is wrapped in dark oak paneling, offering visual contrast to the sun-filled living room and encouraging further exploration through the house, from the entry foyer toward the spaces beyond.

Tucked into the front corner is the main stair to the upper level, with softly shaped Sapele Mahogany treads extending over a shallow pool of water. Lit by a triangular skylight above, the interlocking elements of the feature stair are multiplied in the reflection in the water's surface. Honed stone floors mimic the reflection of the pool, as shimmering natural light is cast on the walls.

A mezzanine overlooks the front landscape and ocean beyond. From this perch, a bridge leads to the home's private wing—a playroom, library, office, three bedrooms, and master suite wrapping around a private courtyard. The surface of this interior terrace is punctuated with organically shaped oculi, which funnel natural light into the garage below.

Within the private courtyard, attention is turned toward two magnificent olive trees. As though the house has been shaped around them, the trees mark the house's zenith—the origin from which the structure gently unfolds down the hill.

The upper level offers transparency and connectivity to the adjacent Topanga State Park and its surrounding landscape. From here, aligning with the axis, one can look through the architecture as a lens. Views compound and blend, thoughtfully framing each moment from the outside to the inside to the outside again.

One can meander with instinctive ease up and through the house, experiencing the harmonic contrasts that orchestrate a rhythmic passage through the interior topography. The protective solidity of the limestone-clad walls alternates with the open and brightly lit spaces defined by expansive views. This cascading sequence of spaces gives the home its poetic rhythm and lends an organic flow to the geometric organization. The exterior views maintain a link with the natural landscape beyond, while the double-height spaces and the feature stair create a vertical and airy feel. Far from being inserted into the landscape, one feels the innate compatibility between the built and the natural, each complementing and enhancing the other.

TRAMONTO DR.
ROBIN @ 3/17/10

4/6/10

TRAMUTO
4/7/10

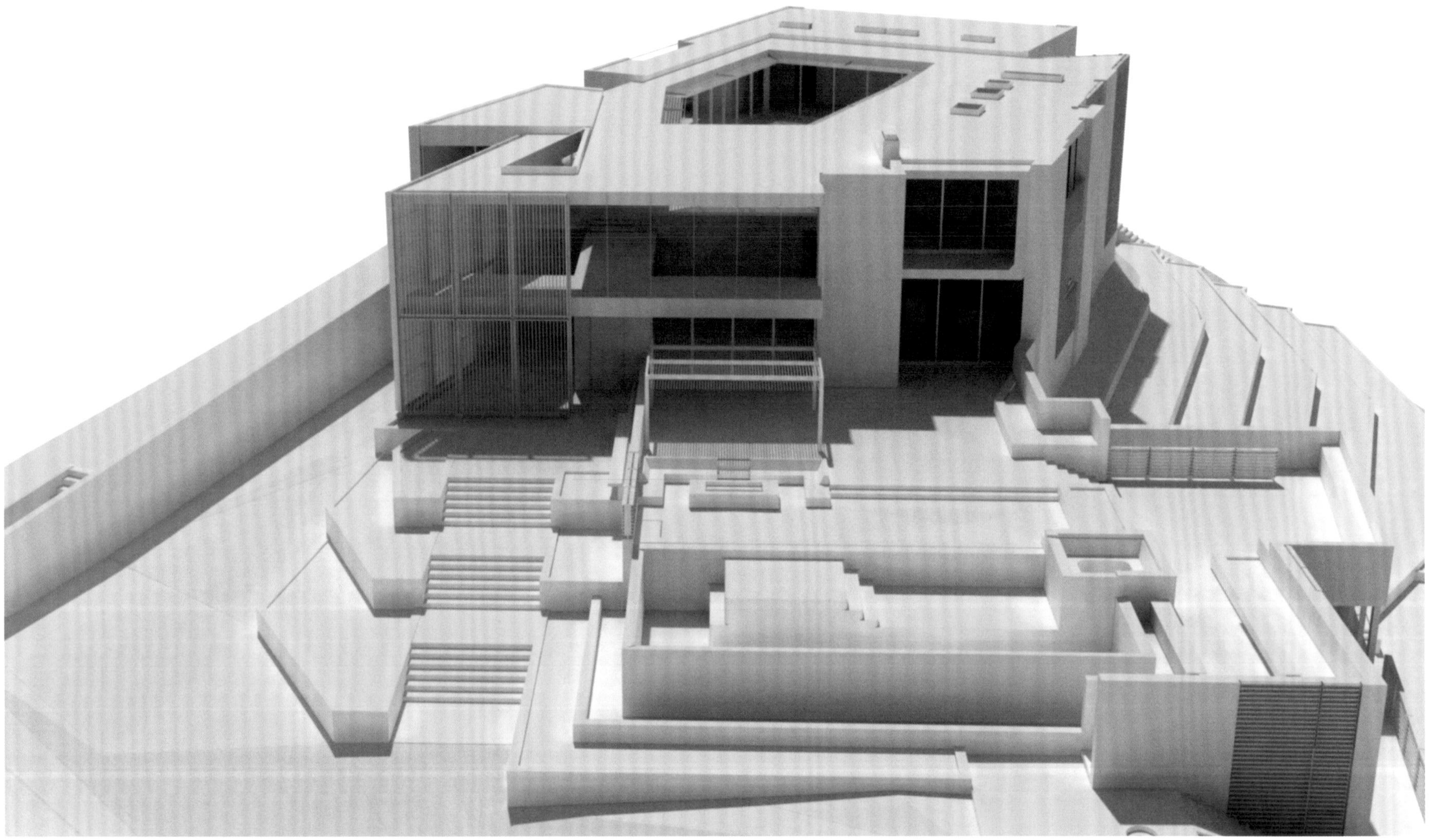

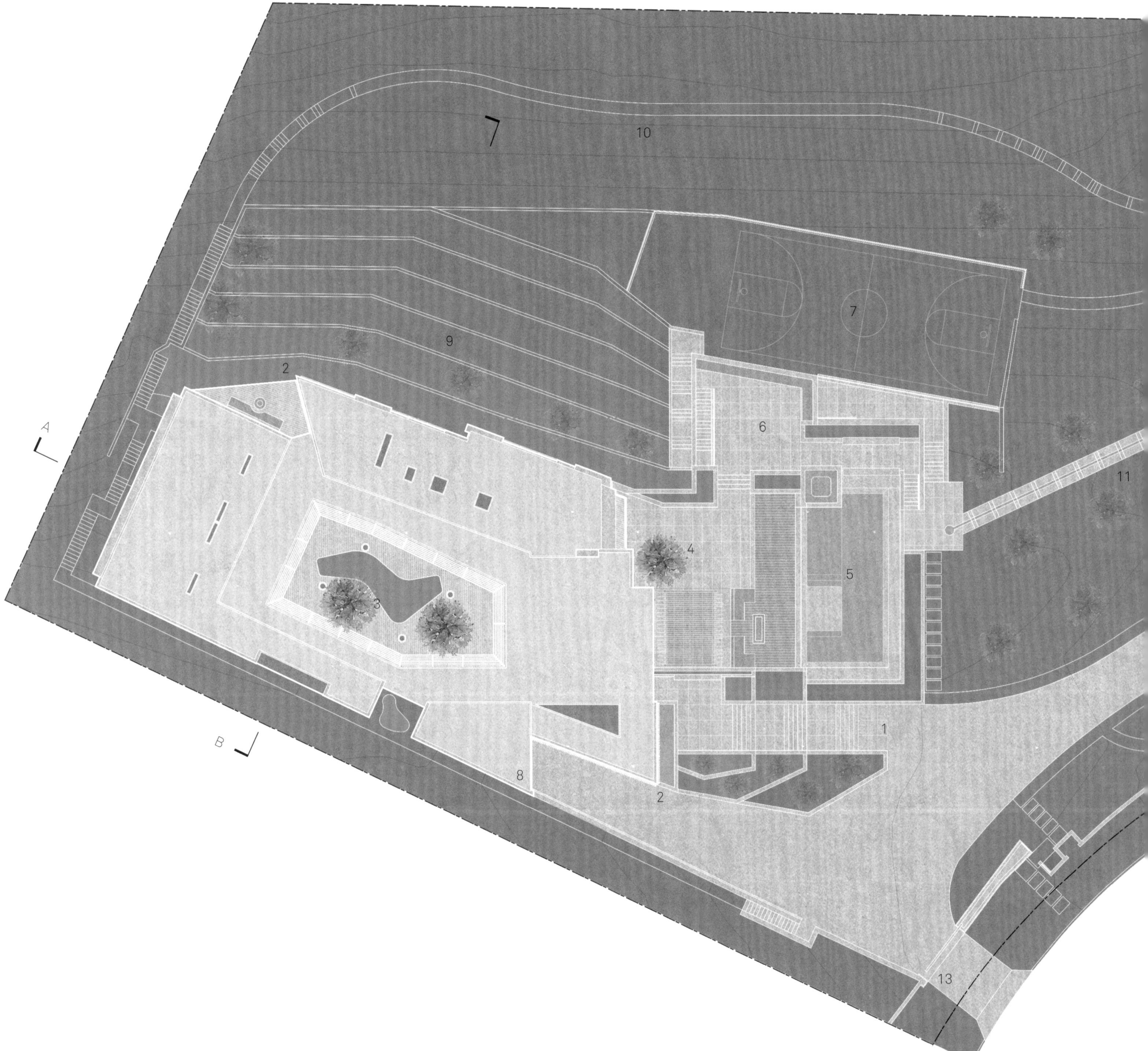

10
7
9
2
6
A
11
4
5
3
1
B
8
2
13

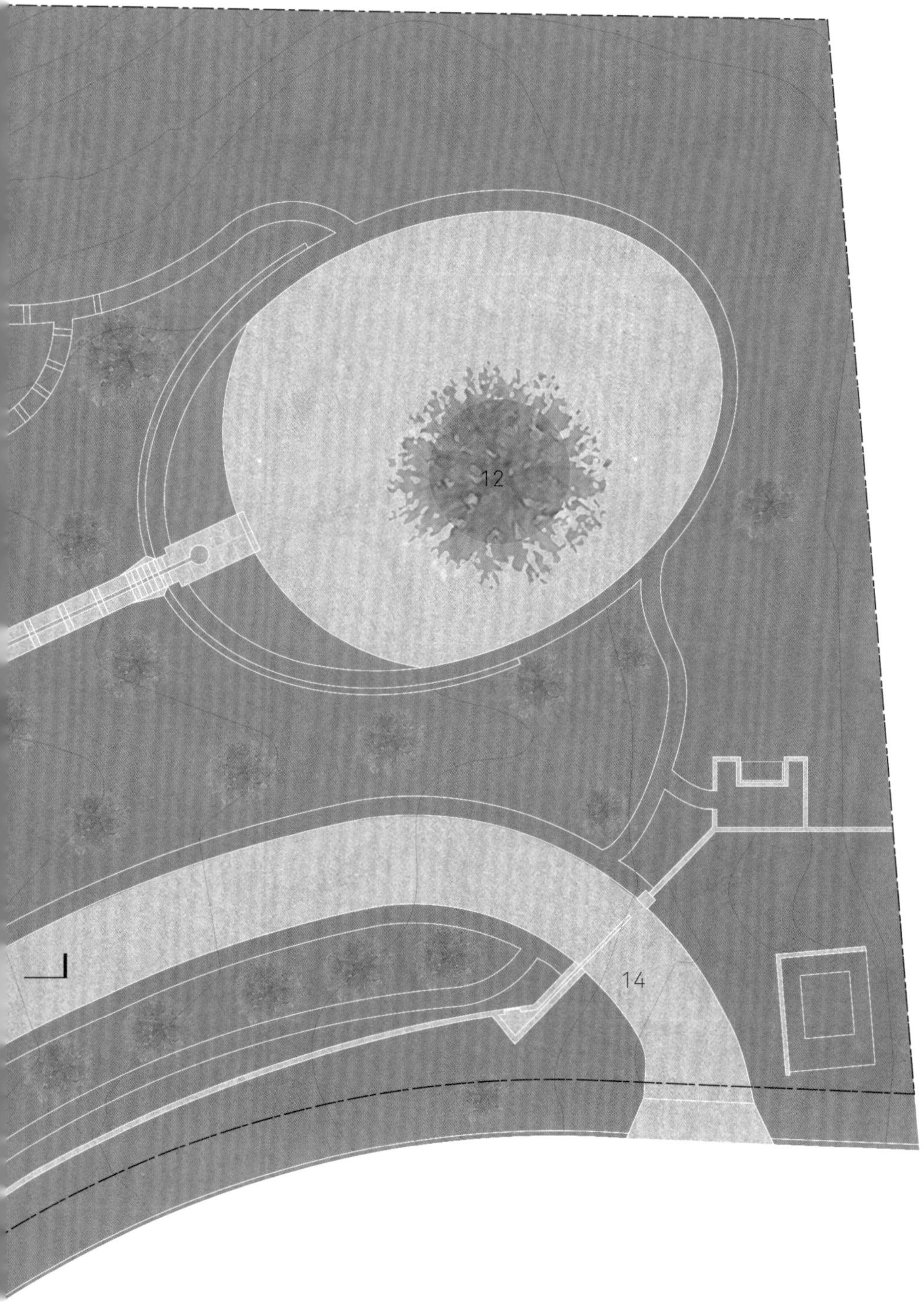

SITE PLAN

1 ENTRY STEPS
2 EXTERIOR SCREENS
3 COURTYARD
4 MAIN TERRACE
5 SWIMMING POOL
6 ACCESSORY BUILDING
7 PLAY COURT
8 GARAGE ENTRANCE
9 TERRACED GARDEN
10 PERIMETER PATH
11 STEPPED WATER RUNNEL
12 FEATURE TREE
13 PRIMARY DRIVEWAY
14 SECONDARY DRIVEWAY

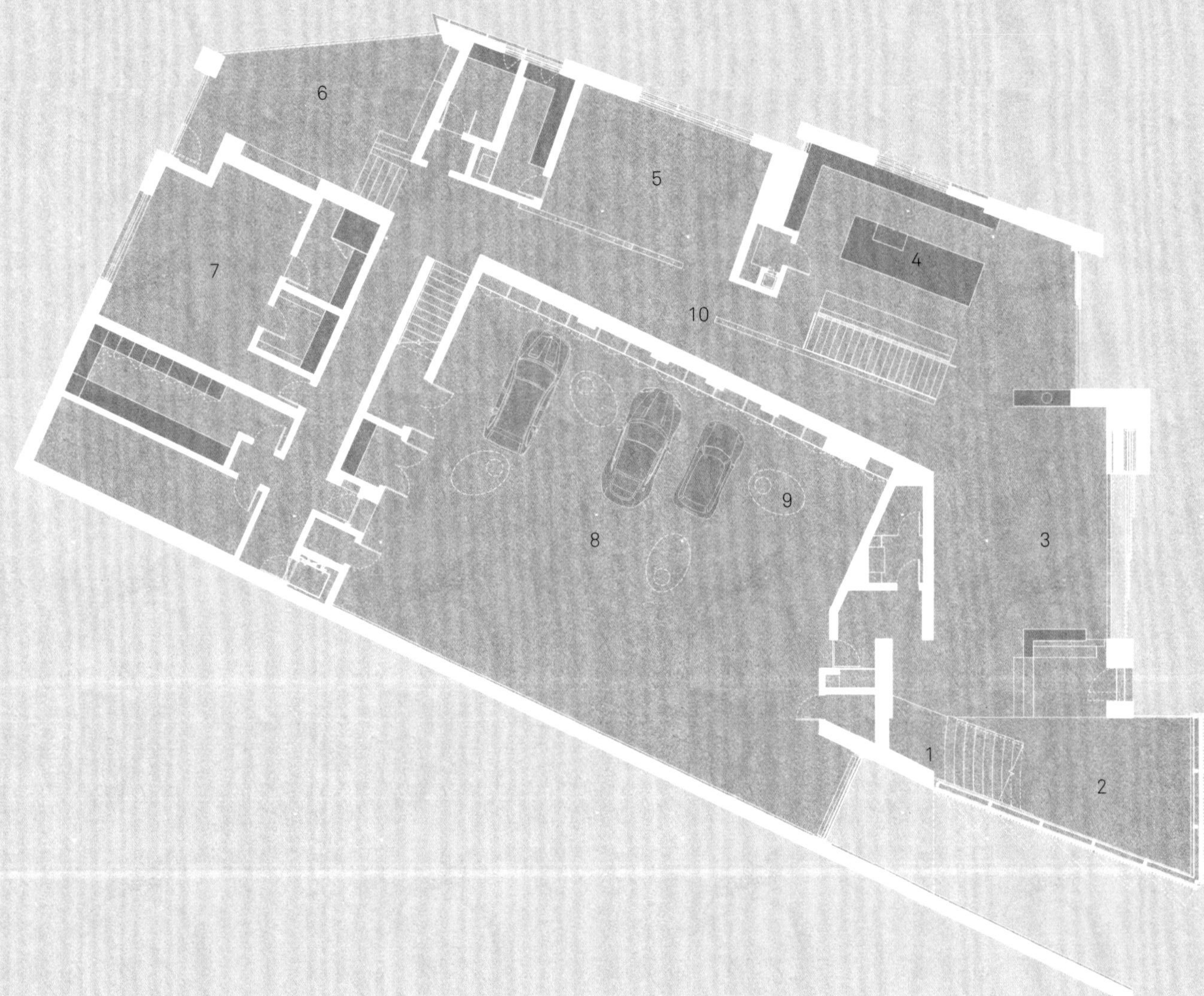

FIRST FLOOR

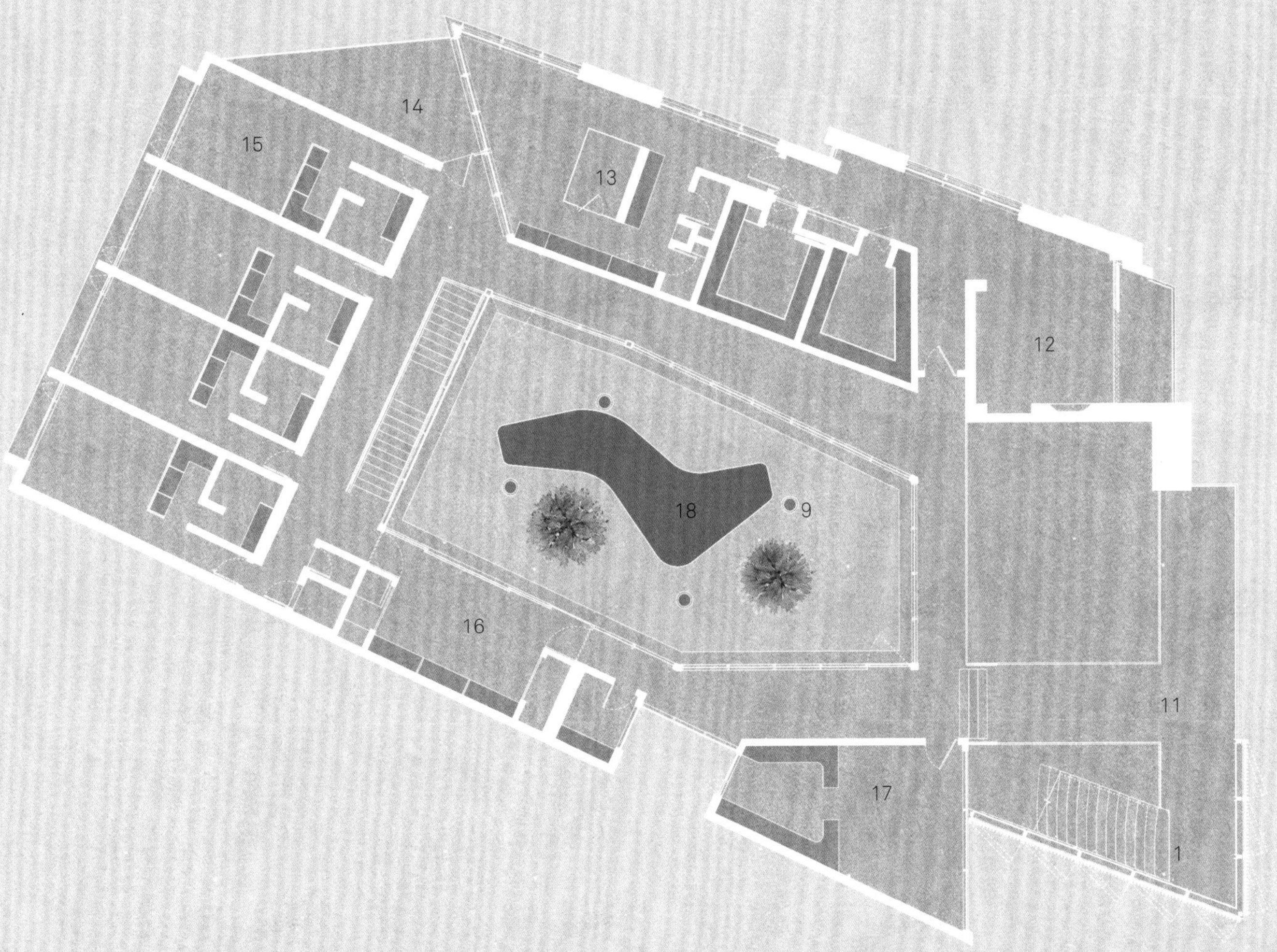

1 FEATURE STAIR
2 REFLECTING POOL
3 MAIN LIVING ROOM
4 KITCHEN
5 DINING ROOM
6 SUNKEN FAMILY ROOM
7 GUEST SUITE
8 GARAGE
9 OCULI
10 INTERIOR SCREEN
11 MEZZANINE / BRIDGE
12 MASTER BEDROOM
13 MASTER BATHROOM
14 OVERLOOK TERRACE
15 BEDROOMS
16 PLAYROOM
17 LIBRARY / OFFICE
18 UPPER COURTYARD

SECOND FLOOR

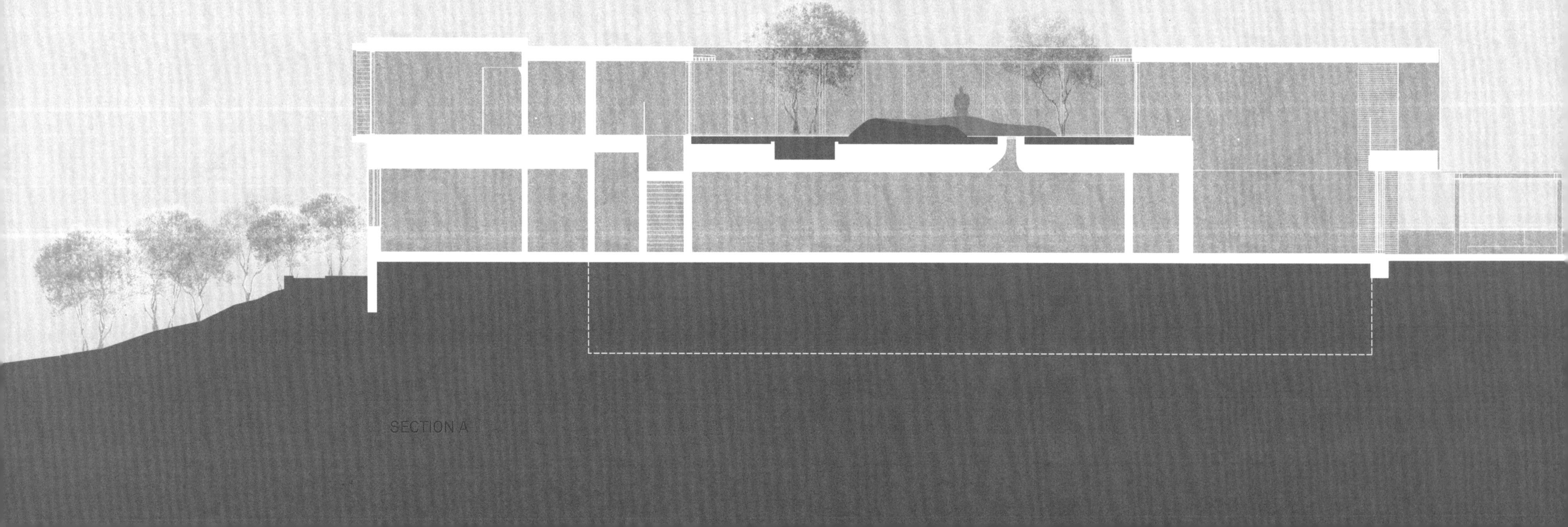

SECTION A

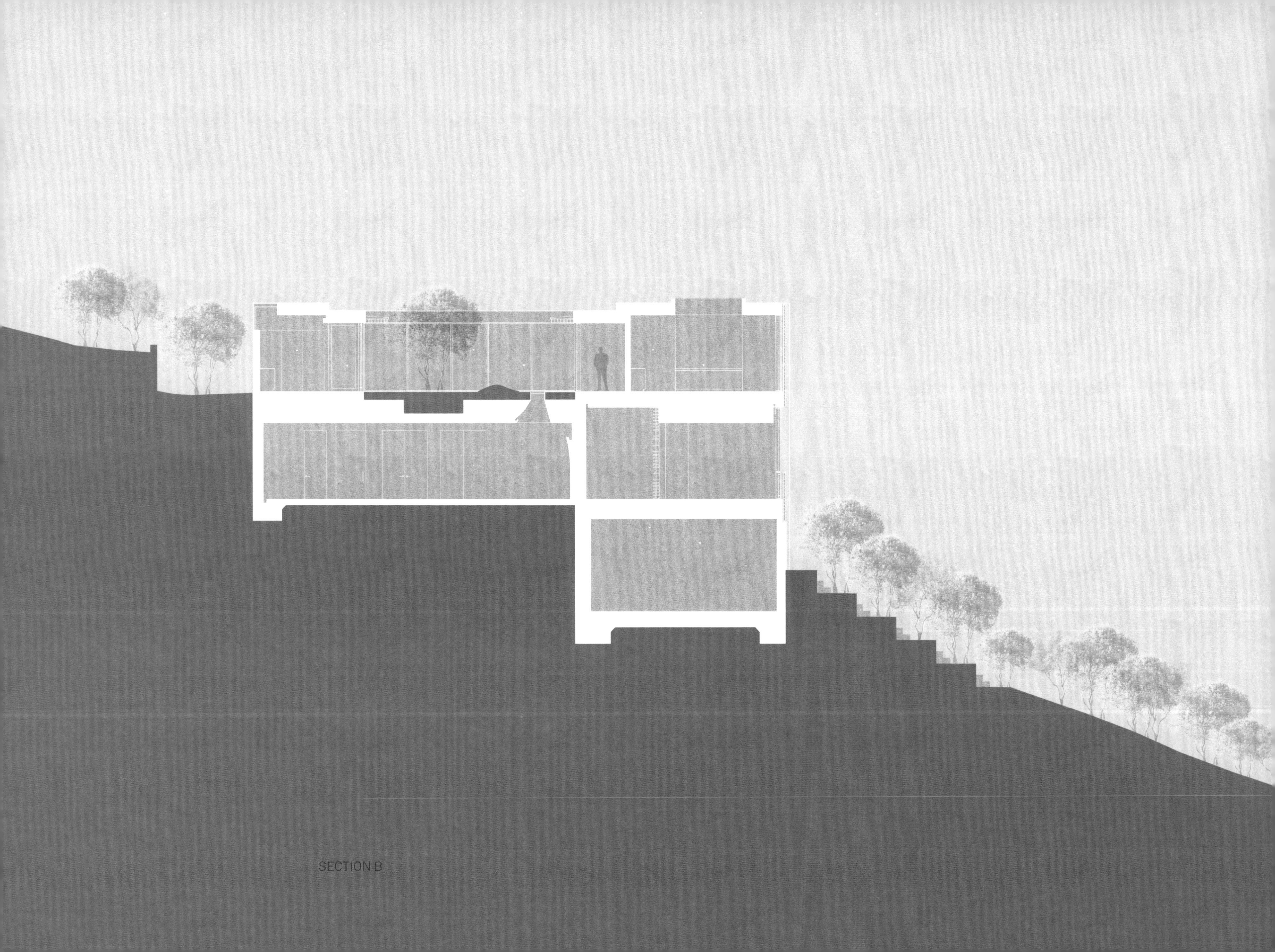

SECTION B

WRIGHT
WRIGHT
Leonardo da Vinci

METHODS + MAKING

Research and development are integral to our design process. We dedicate time and intention to understand the site and project-specific conditions as rigorously as possible. This approach offers the opportunity to study the project both functionally and formally, including how light interacts with the site, how a specific material may enhance or detract from the experience of the space, which facade system is best suited, and how each project connects with the personal narrative of our clients. Our creative experimentation begins with open-ended curiosity at times, and in other instances, our research emerges upon encountering challenges that require further investigation. These processes and resulting designs help push our practice forward and acknowledge the fundamental importance of the human endeavor in architecture.

In siting the Tramonto Residence and its formal arrangements, we encountered several areas that compelled unique and customized solutions. Engaging these moments as opportunities for innovation and connection with the client's specific needs allowed our design process to iterate and evolve specific elements to inform the home's overall geometry and vice versa.

These design solutions were thoroughly vetted and refined over an extensive development period, including physical models and prototypes. For several key elements, full-scale mockups enabled us to refine our study of the experiential dimension of the house. The resulting details becoming the anchoring elements, thoughtful moments choreographed to amplify the experience of moving through and between spaces.

FILTER

Due to the intensity of the Southern California sun, glare and shading were essential considerations. For the facade, a partial envelope of operable exterior wood and steel screens was developed to mitigate the sun's heat and add warmth and contrast to the limestone and glass.

Near the main entrance, operable two-story vertical screens wrap the corner, carefully designed to withstand the wracking forces of hinged operation and minimize movement in the wooden elements. The size of steel members and support elements were studied through detailed drawings and 3D models to resolve complex intersections, operable components, and adjacent relationships.

We fabricated an operable full-scale mockup of a vertical screen to test the performance of these components, which were critical in developing the necessary details. The constructive aspects of the vertical screens informed the design of the relatively small-scale horizontal screens used elsewhere on the facade. A second full-scale mockup was built to study and test their lateral movement, electronic control, size of actuator struts, and related mechanical detailing.

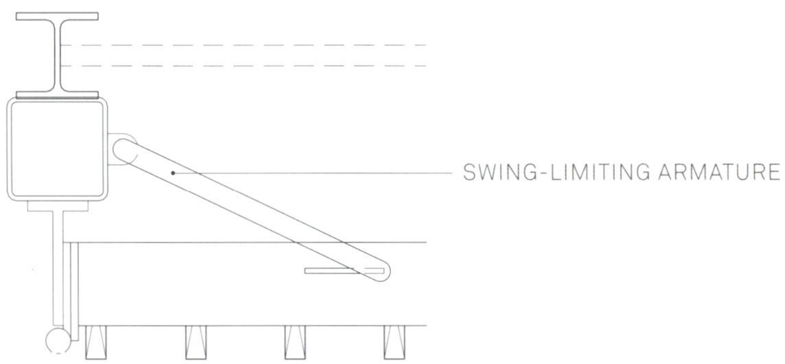

PLAN AT SWING LIMITER

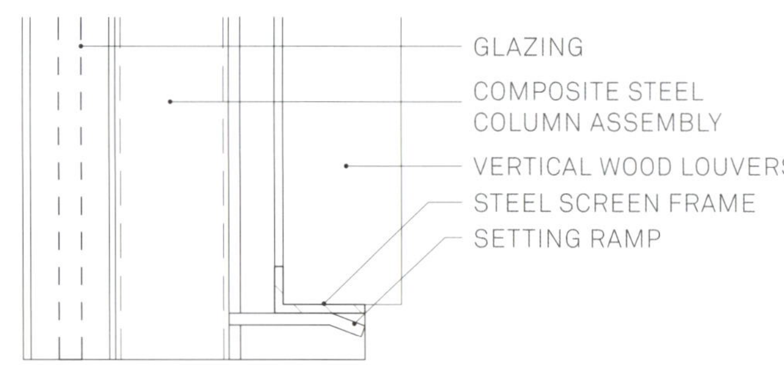

SILL DETAIL

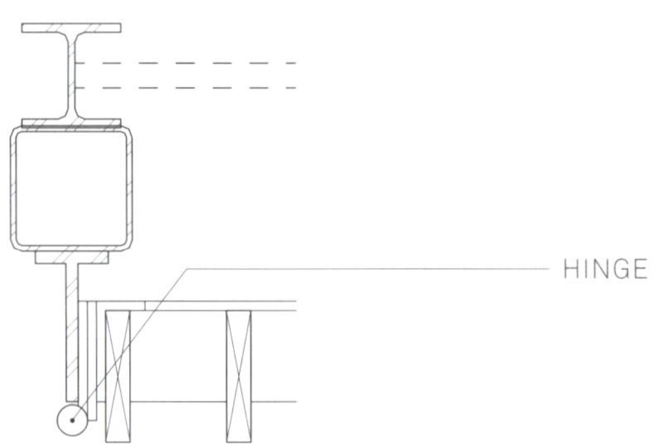

PLAN AT HINGE

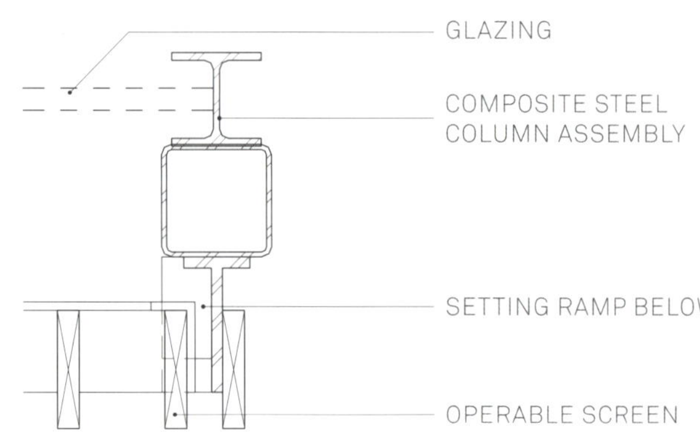

PLAN AT SWING END

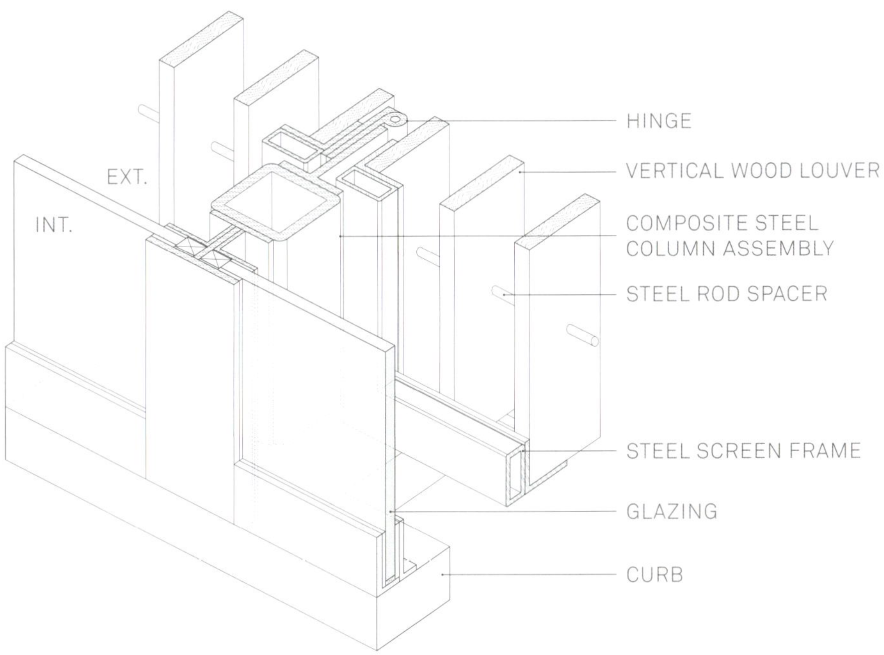
HINGE
VERTICAL WOOD LOUVER
EXT.
INT.
COMPOSITE STEEL
COLUMN ASSEMBLY
STEEL ROD SPACER
STEEL SCREEN FRAME
GLAZING
CURB

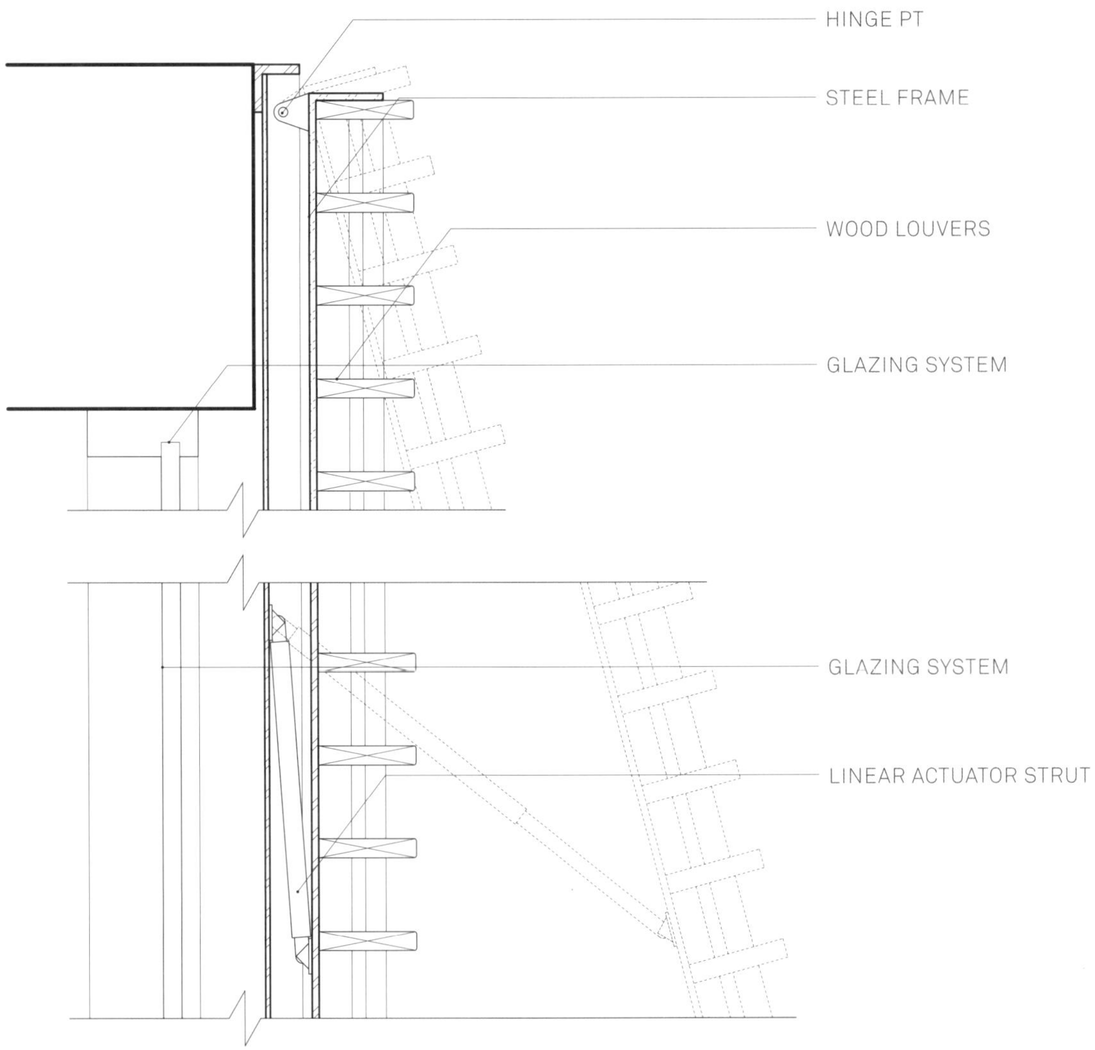

OPERABLE SCREEN DETAILS

PLAN AT OPERABLE SCREEN JAMB

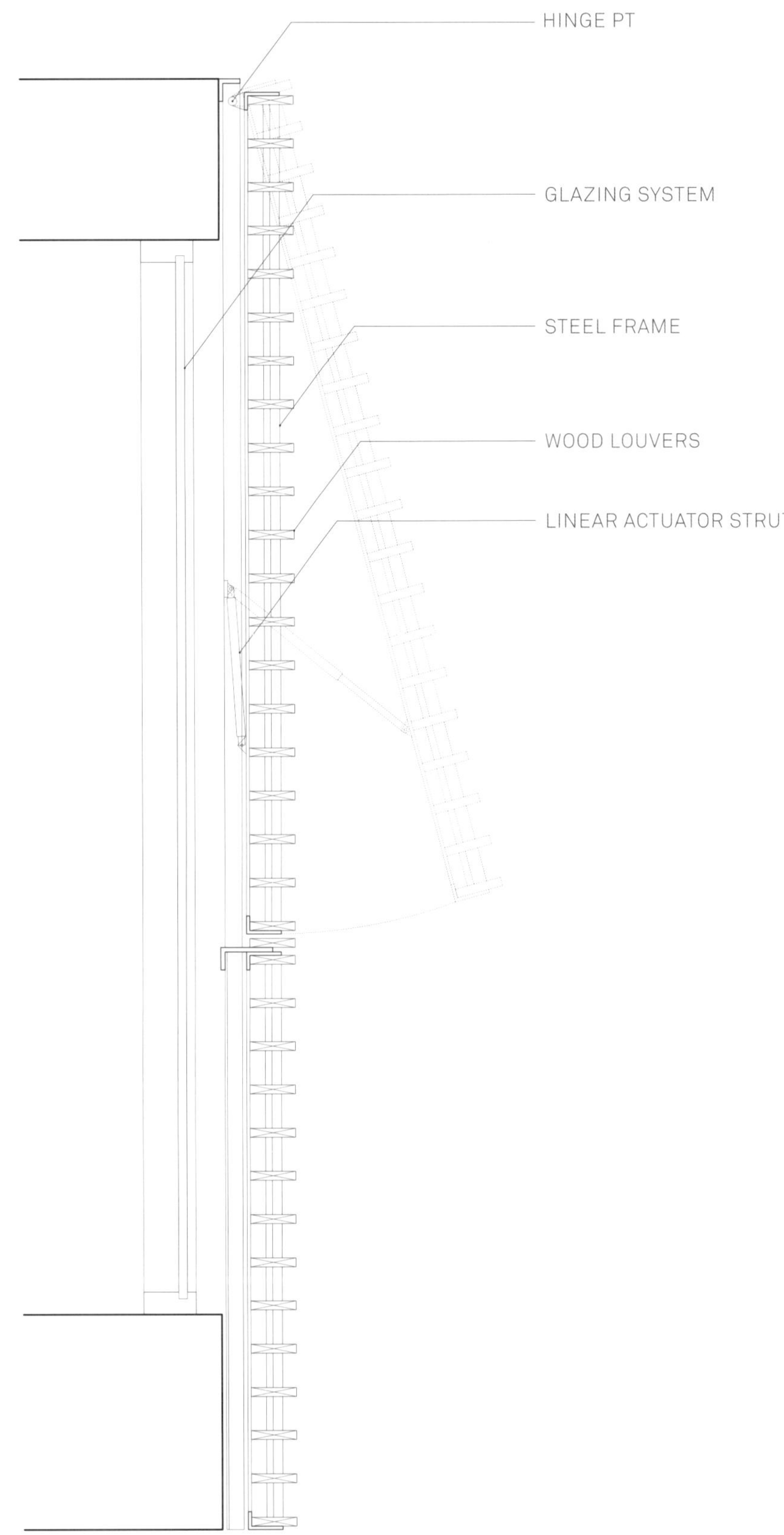

OPERABLE SCREEN ASSEMBLY

ASCEND

A feature stair leading to the house's upper level provides a signature element anchoring the entry experience inside the home. Adjacent to the entrance foyer, the stair triangulates a mezzanine space and upper bridge rising above a reflecting pool. Initially envisaged as an exterior stair, freestanding with a formally expressive underside, the stair later evolved into an integral interior form, beautifully filtering light over a shallow pool of water. In this way, the shaping of the stair is intimately tied to the overlapping geometries of the house, its angles addressing the site's forces and determining the exterior envelope of the structure.

As the stair became more expressive, we found opportunities to develop its tectonic and material qualities. A rigorous study of the stair-tread began with hand sketches of the initial form, supported along the glass edge. A row of suspended and darkened steel rods supplemented lateral support on the cantilevered end, acting as the required guardrail. Initial studies honed into the elemental form, leading to physical models that explored the interlocking relationship among the pieces.

Milled from laminated pieces of solid Sapele Mahogany, the stair's 19 cantilevered treads explore the concept of a series of repeated forms that gain compounded structural integrity through their interlocking arrangement. The carved wood treads are fluted in profile, subtly tapering along their length and adding an organic subtext to the architecture's dialogue.

In selecting the stair materials, we discovered an opportunity to connect with the clients' unique story and consider the structural parameters. Our material studies and design iterations presented different options, including cast terrazzo and various wood species. We tested the design surface, grain continuity, and the material's ability to integrate internal structural elements. Through a process of scaled physical models, we determined that seven layers of vertically laminated solid Sapele Mahogany suited the technical conditions best. This selection offered the desired material richness to complement the surrounding wooden screens, lending a warm and luxurious distinction to the stone floor and adjacent walls.

Full-sized, 3-dimensional foam mockups were milled for design review with the client and to test the accurate perceptual and experiential scale while simultaneously ensuring optimal support sizing and spans. Several other custom details were developed, including a "capo" device to minimize lateral vibration in the vertically hung steel rods, cast brass infill elements, and a bespoke wood-and-steel handrail.

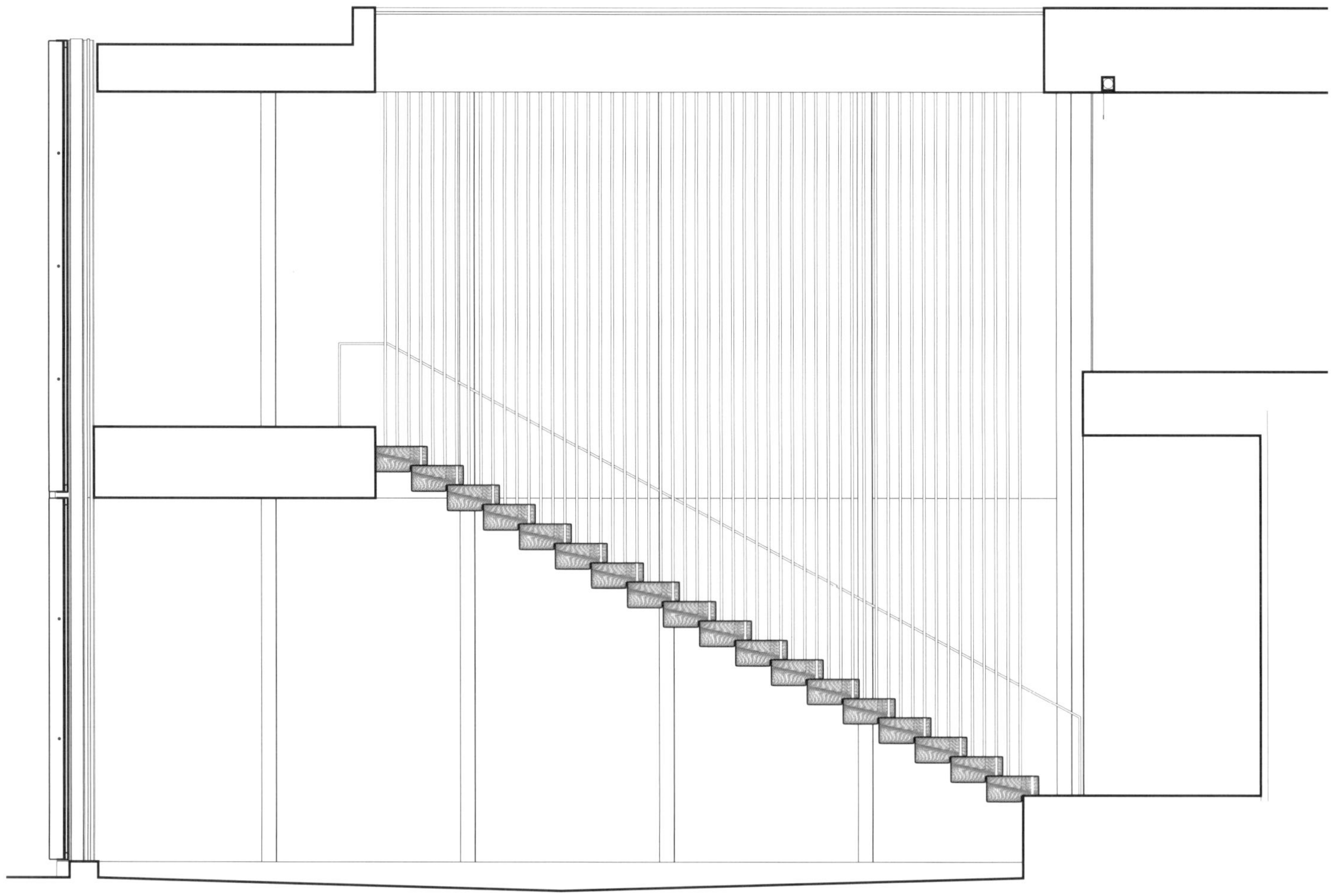

STAIR ELEVATION

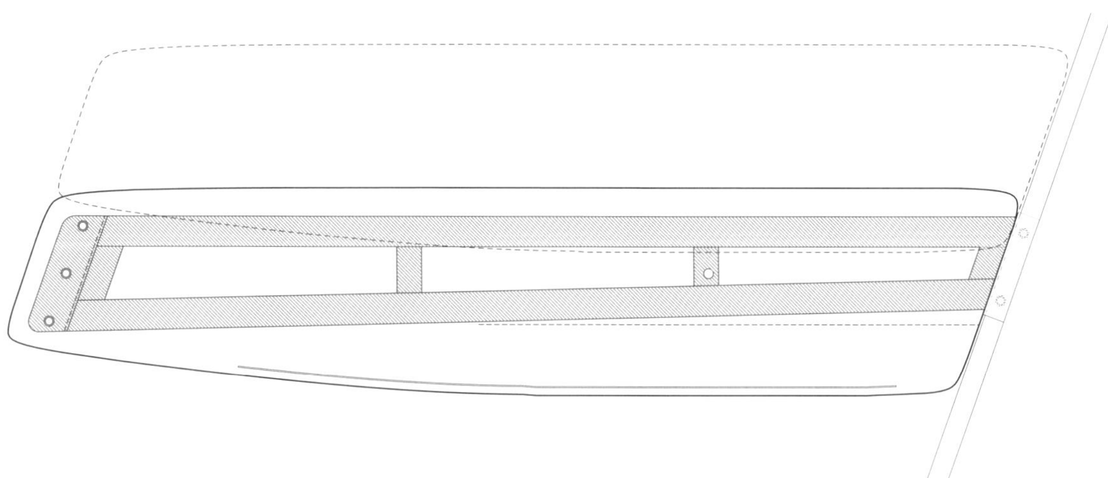

PLAN AT STAIR TREAD

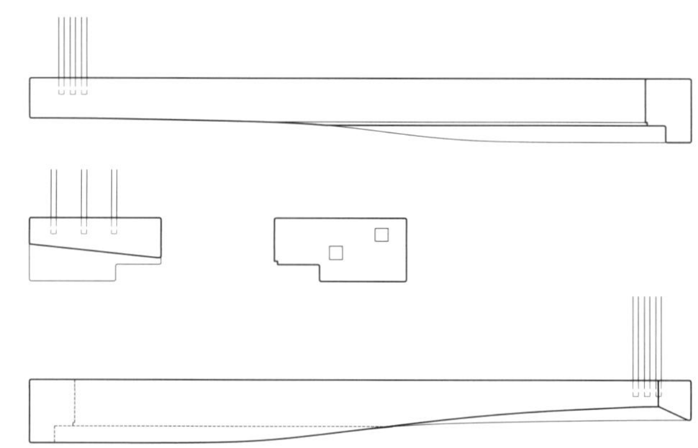

STAIR TREAD ELEVATIONS

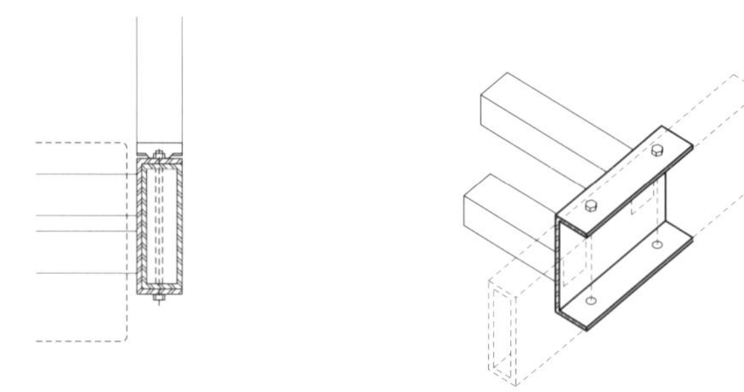

STAIR STRINGER DETAILS

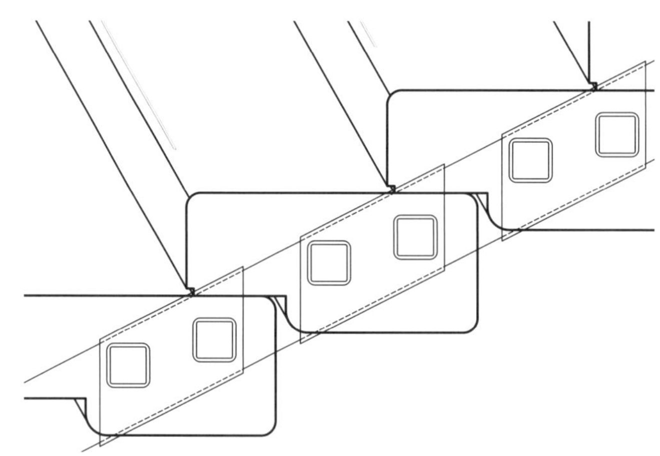

STAIR SECTION

VEIL

The linearity and repetition of forms defining the feature stair are reflected in a system of interior louvered screens functioning as a spatial dividing element. Carved from the same Sapele Mahogany, these screens shape the formal dining room while vertically connecting the basement stair to the rest of the residence above and serving as the stair's guardrail.

The screen's textural pattern offers a sense of visual porosity, maintaining natural light penetration into the corridor and implying a degree of spatial separation. The screens are offset in two sections angled from the axis of the space to punctuate the corridor's perceived length and shape, offering a layered perspective through the latticework. The two offset sections also frame the uninterrupted view from the home's front to the family room at the opposite end.

Each louver is carefully crafted with a tapering profile that amplifies a three-dimensional experience by allowing natural light to linger on the softened surfaces. All the outer edges are eased to heighten their tactility and enhance visual warmth throughout. The level of resolution between the stained-wood louvers and the vertical darkened-steel supports is composed in a layered dialogue with the larger-scale operations and geometries present throughout the residence. These interior screens share a material and formal language with the exterior screen facade, extending their relationship throughout the design.

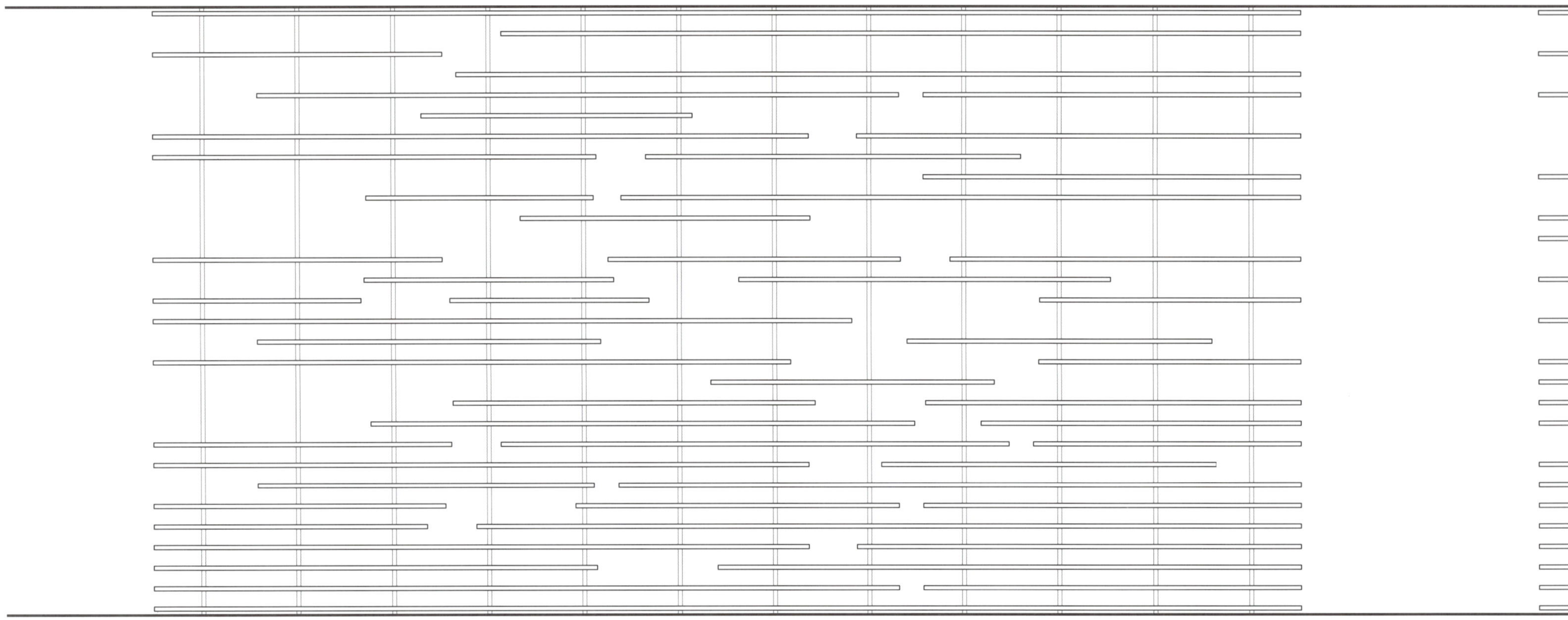

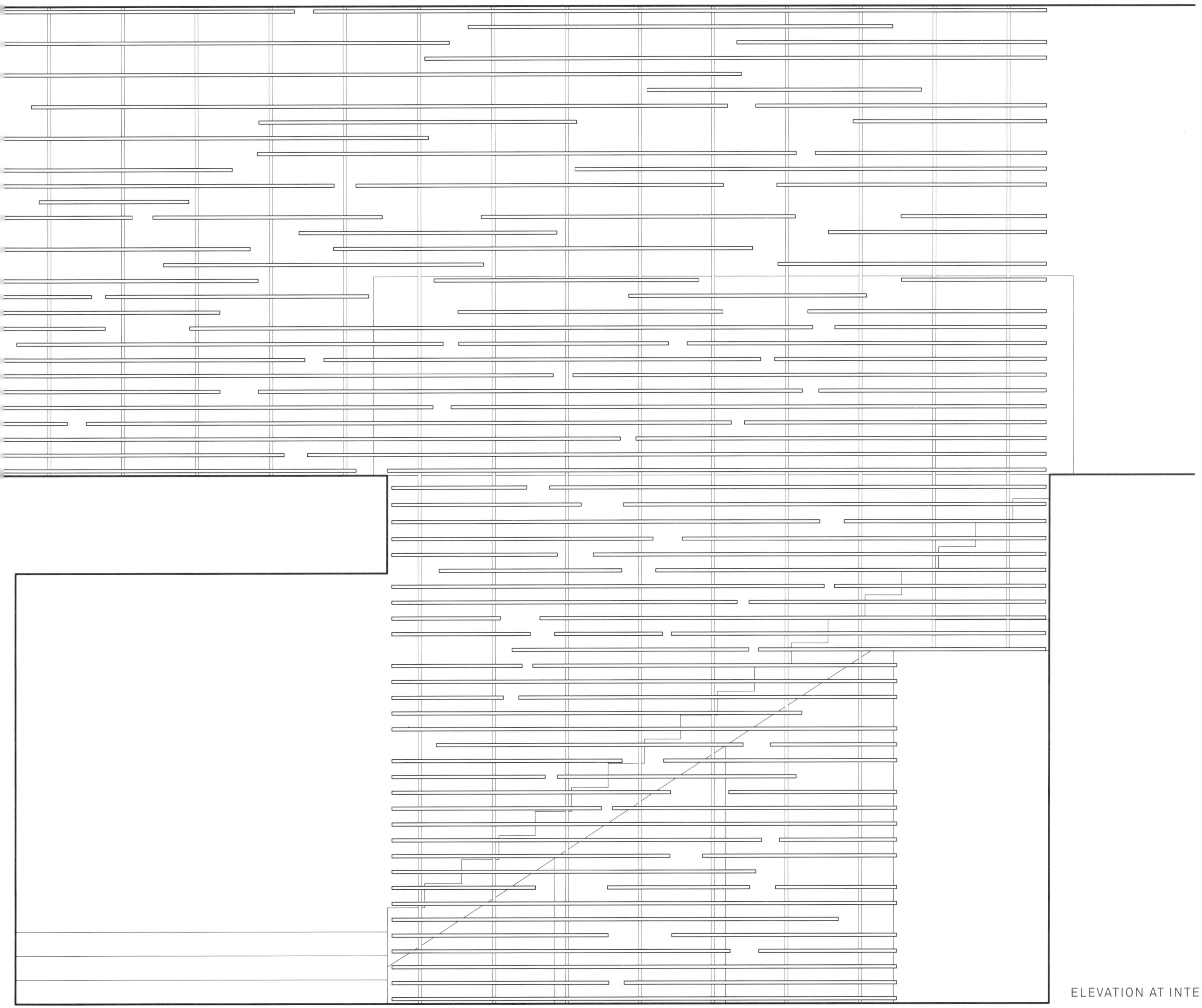

ELEVATION AT INTERIOR SCREEN

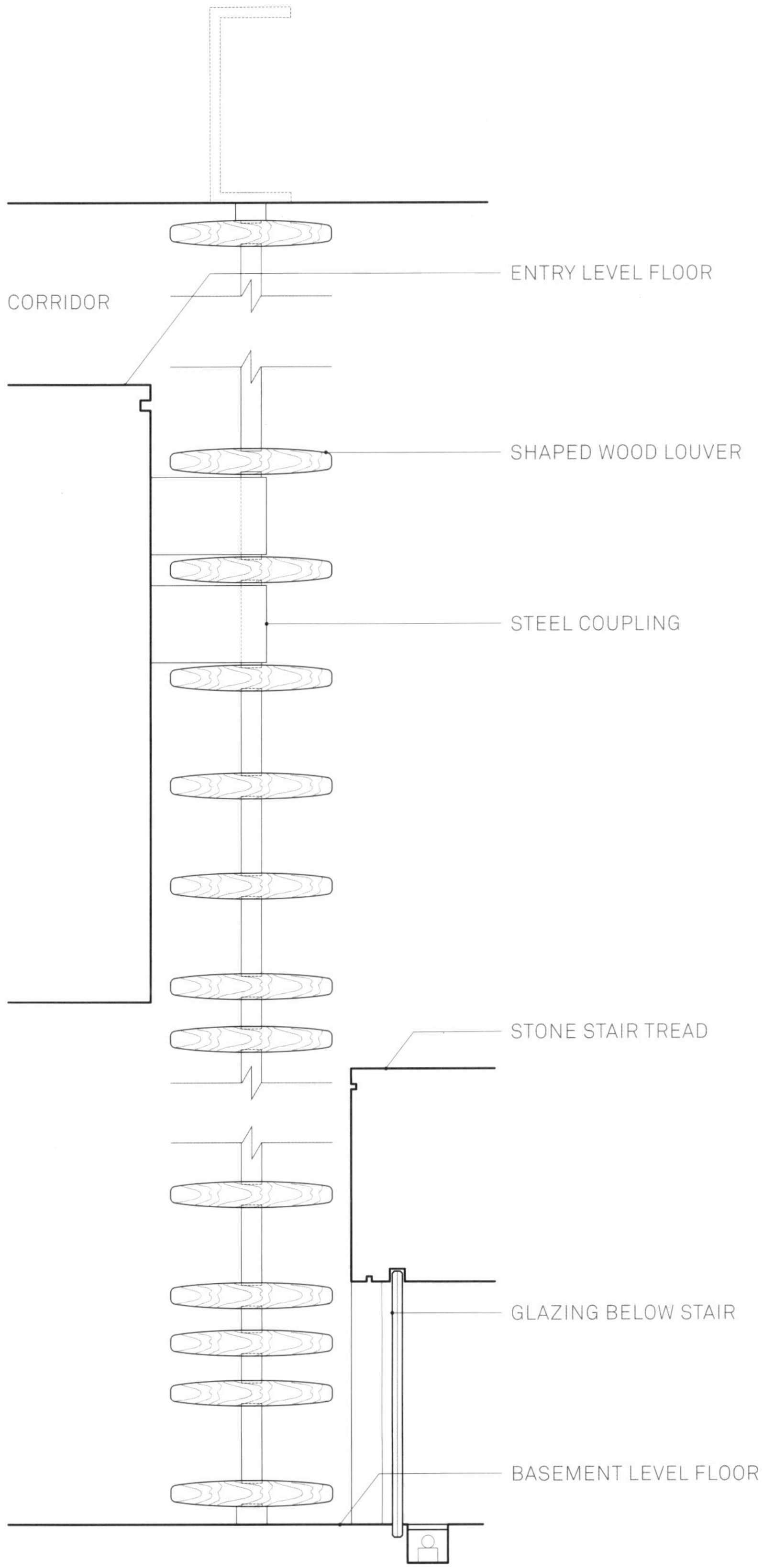

INTERIOR SCREEN ASSEMBLY

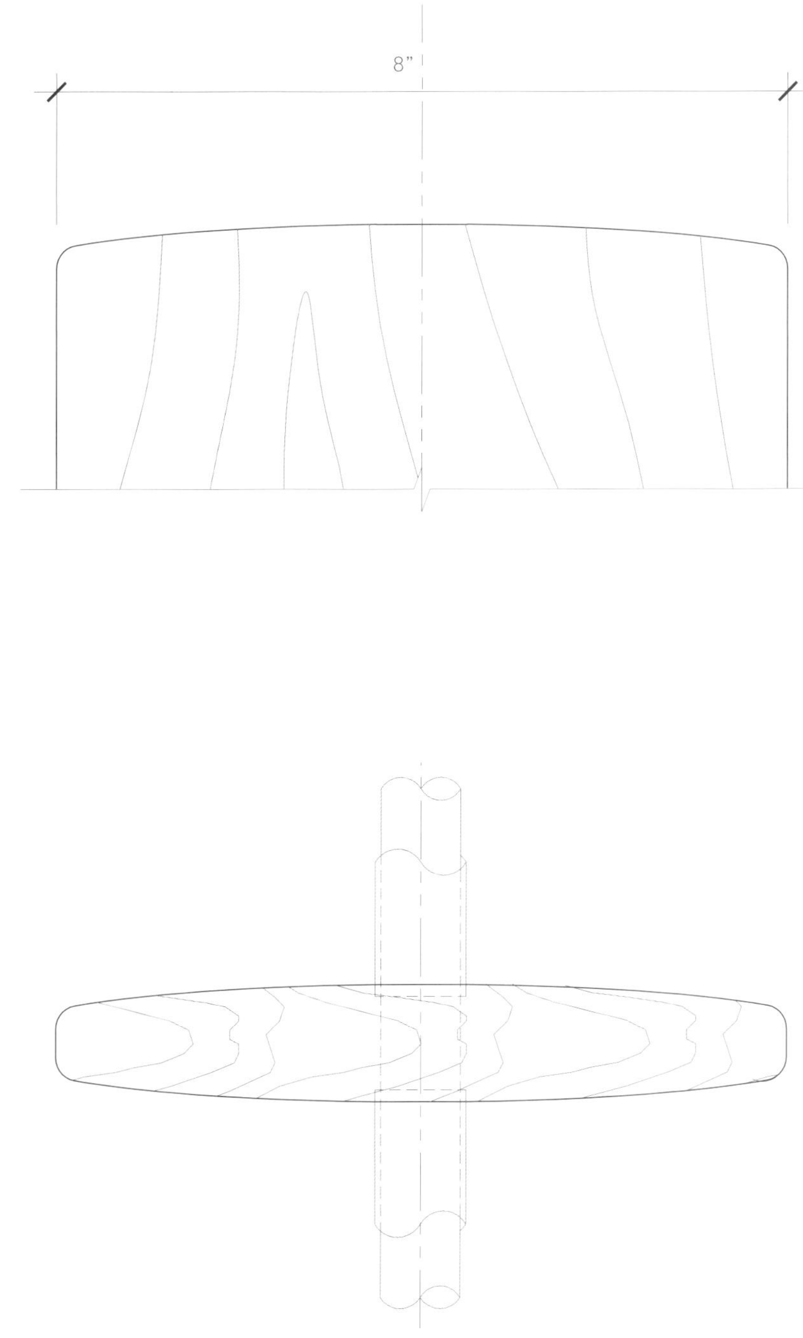

LOUVER ASSEMBLY

ANCHOR

The house is set against the hillside to facilitate the property's circulation and maintain an open and unobstructed connection with the surrounding landscape. Embedding the garage within the residence's interior enables the ground-level spaces to organize themselves without impacting the overall massing. The arrangement of the living spaces around the garage provides a direct connection between the spaces while preserving the canyon and ocean views.

A private outdoor courtyard above the garage allows the surrounding nature to flow around and through the residence, merging the built form with the natural terrain, a central intention of the project. The creative coordination of structural beams enables the presence of the two mature olive trees in the courtyard, alongside other planted features. These results are an extension of the natural landscape embedded within the home, providing direct interior and exterior landscaped views to the private upper-level spaces.

Due to this vertical alignment, an opportunity for daylight to sectionally pierce the upper courtyard to the garage below is leveraged using a series of walkable skylights. Set flush with the courtyard deck above, this family of ocular openings generously shares natural light from the planted courtyard with the garage below.

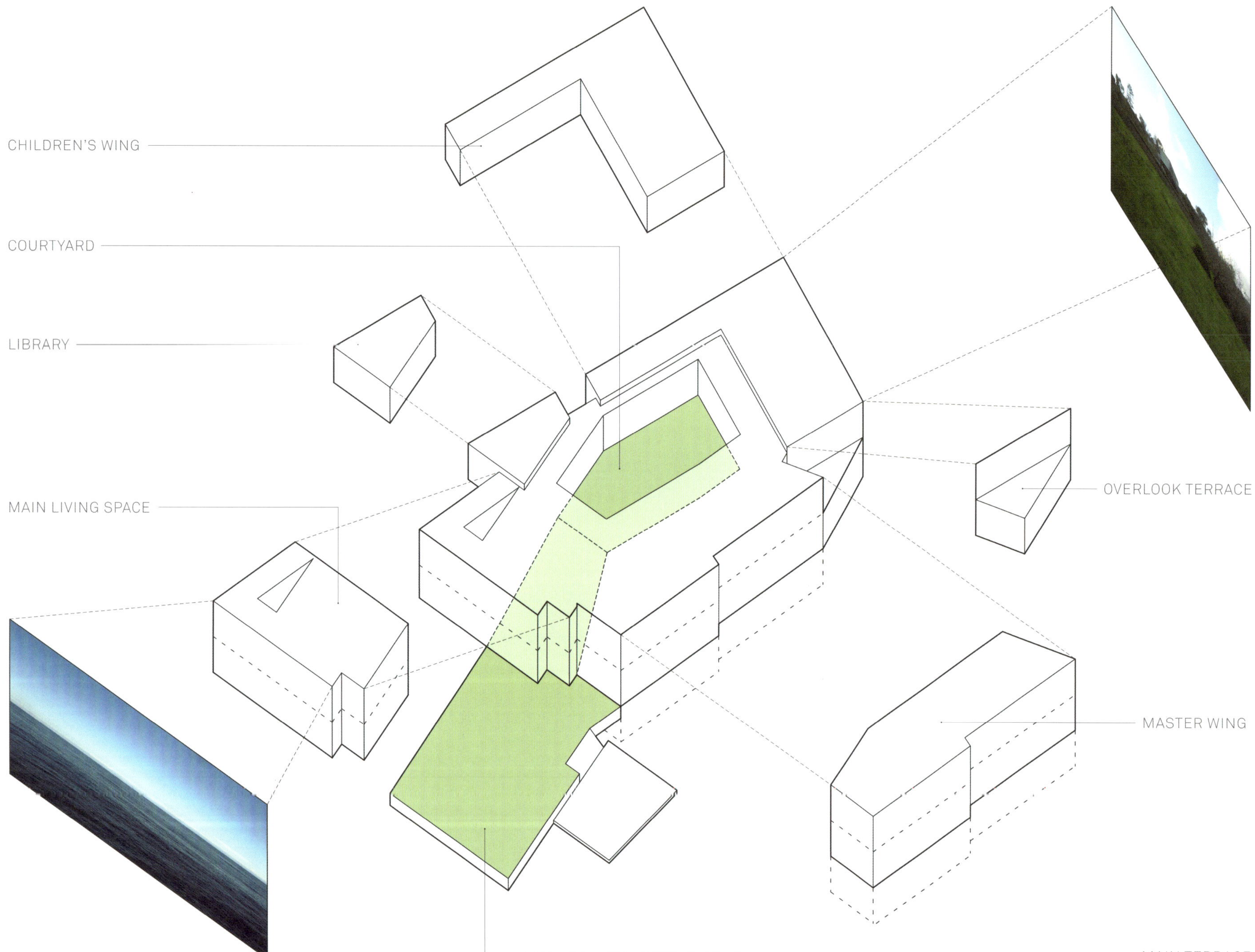
CHILDREN'S WING
COURTYARD
LIBRARY
MAIN LIVING SPACE
OVERLOOK TERRACE
MASTER WING
MAIN TERRACE

OCULI

Four custom oculus skylights allow natural light to filter between the upper courtyard and the garage space below. During the day, the skylights enable the sunlight to penetrate to the lower level. At night, they supplement the soft down-lighting for the garage and an up-lighting glow in the courtyard above.

The skylights are composed of 36-inch (diameter) discs of triple-laminated, textured, and walkable glass set flush with the courtyard's wooden deck. As they pierce the surface toward the space below, the skylights translate into larger, elliptically shaped openings, allowing natural light to expand and activate the garage's ceiling plane.

Interior lighting studies determined the optimal amount of light, glare, and shadow, which informed the ultimate sizing and structural layout of the openings. Sketch studies, 3D models, and mockups led to a split-shell assembly fabricated from glass-fiber-reinforced gypsum that could be fabricated off-site. Once in place, the forms were skimmed with a smooth coat of plaster terminating in an eyelid with a glowing edge enhancing its night-lit character.

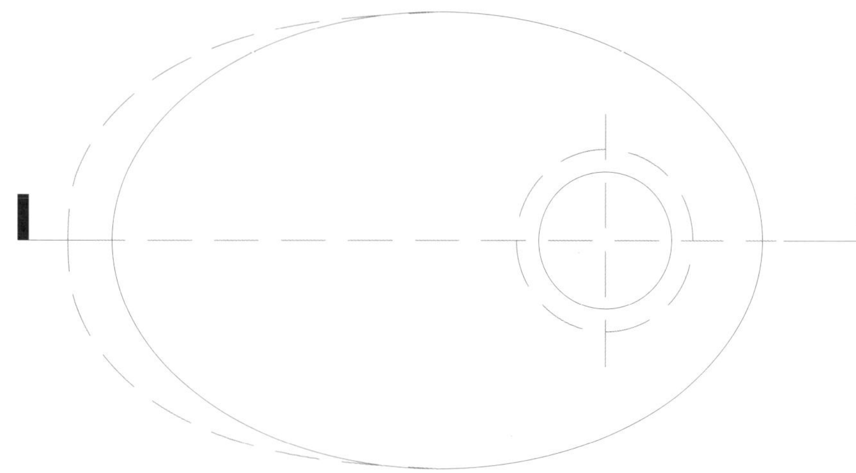

SKYLIGHT PLAN

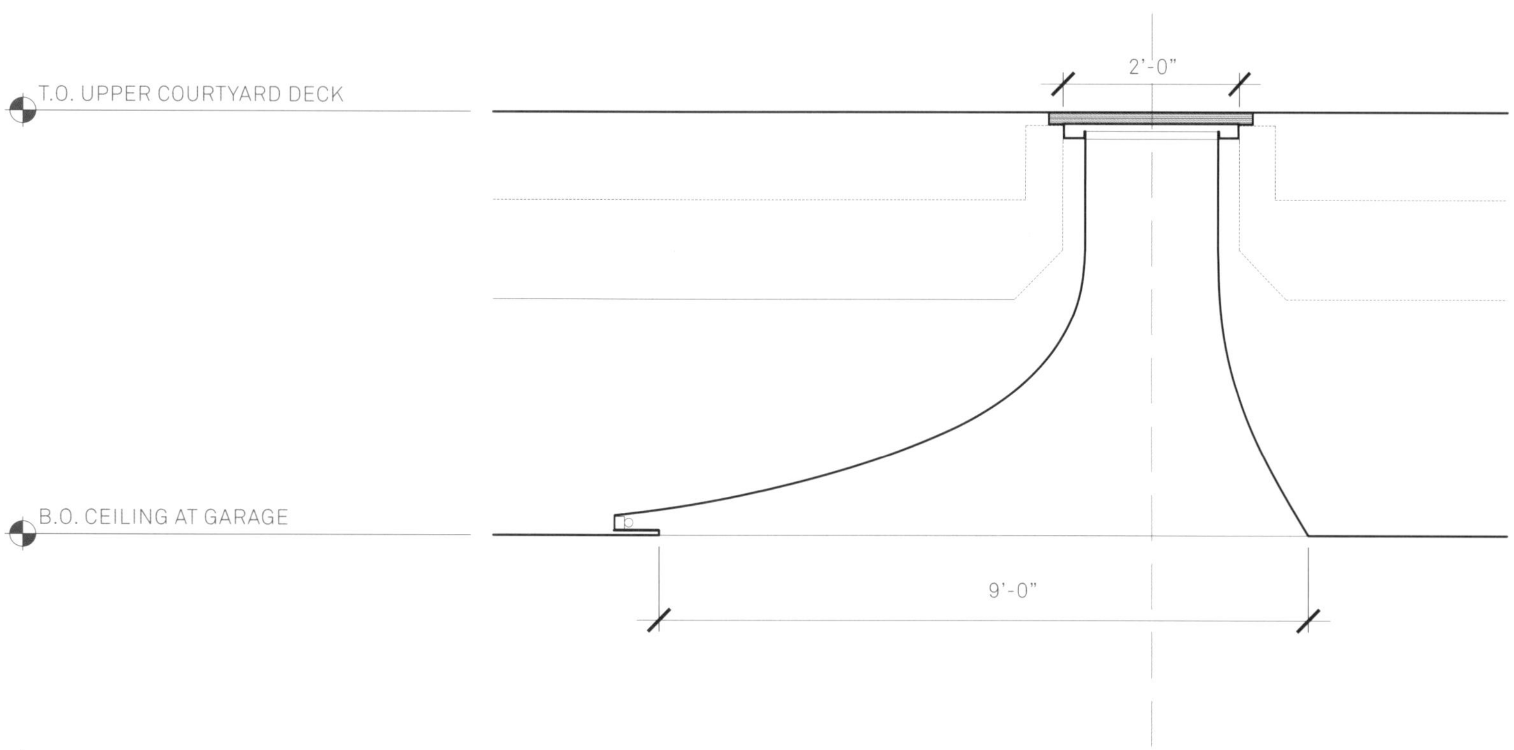

SKYLIGHT SECTION

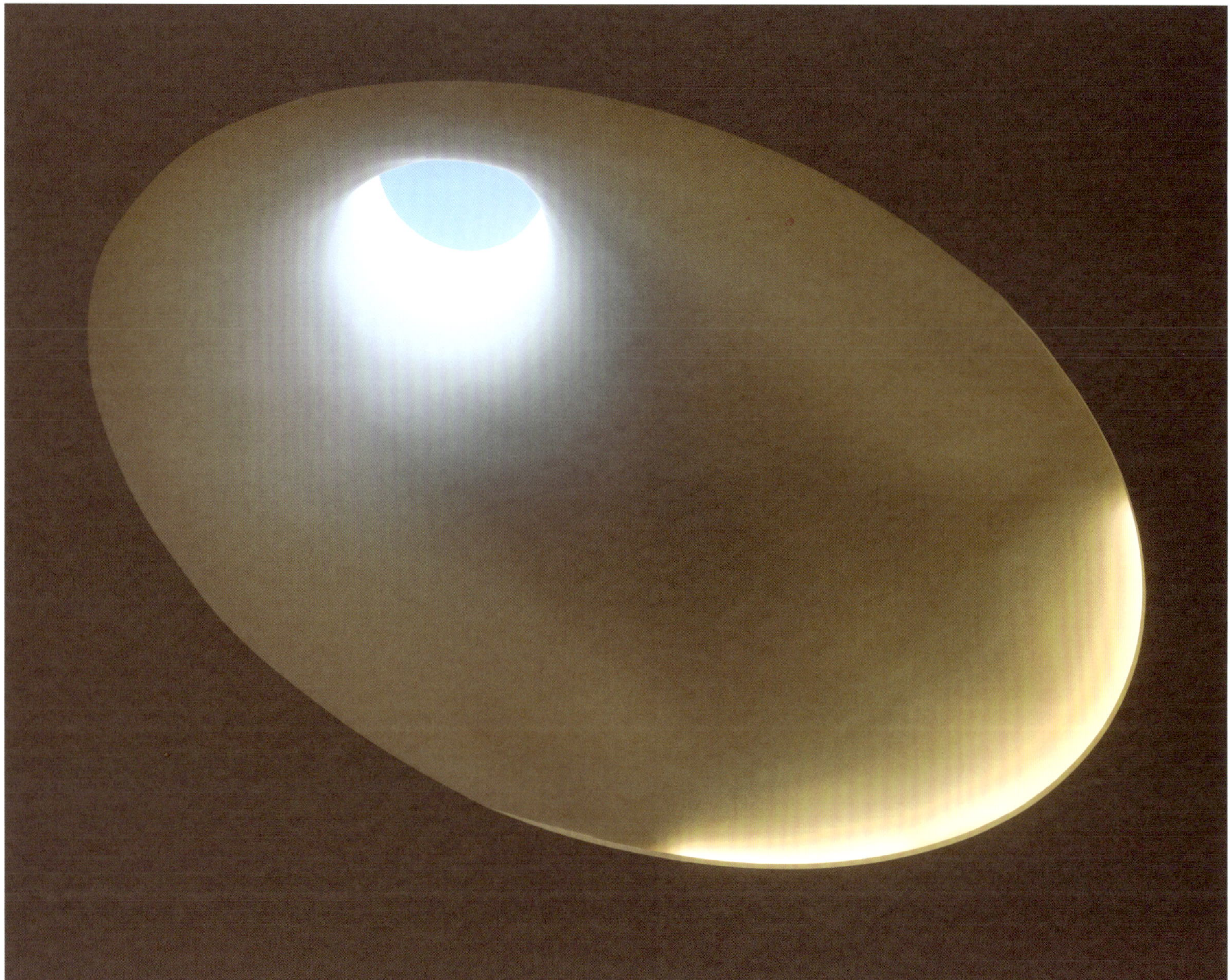

MASKING

The Tramonto drawings by Robin Donaldson, AIA, began as an opportunity to survey a finished piece of architecture as a means to produce a new series of drawings. This sensibility illustrates the understanding that drawings and buildings play a non-linear role in pushing the design practice forward and acknowledges that the design does not end once construction is complete. Throughout the process of making these drawings, we looked at different forms of representation that led to the construction of the architecture. Whether it was a diagram from a concept or a digital model from the construction documents, all forms of representation—analog and digital—presented equal opportunities to influence the evolution of the drawings.

Screen-printing became an essential technique for the construction of the drawings, permitting both the large-scale representation (40" x 60") of playfully collaged technical drawings and the improvisational "artist's hand" to be aesthetically involved directly in the process. The act of drawing and constructing the drawings became inter-dependent, a testament to the practice of design at different scales, accentuating the relationship between architecture and the practice of drawing. This self-referential sensibility propelled these drawings toward unique reflections of the Tramonto Residence and presented new perspectives for future work.

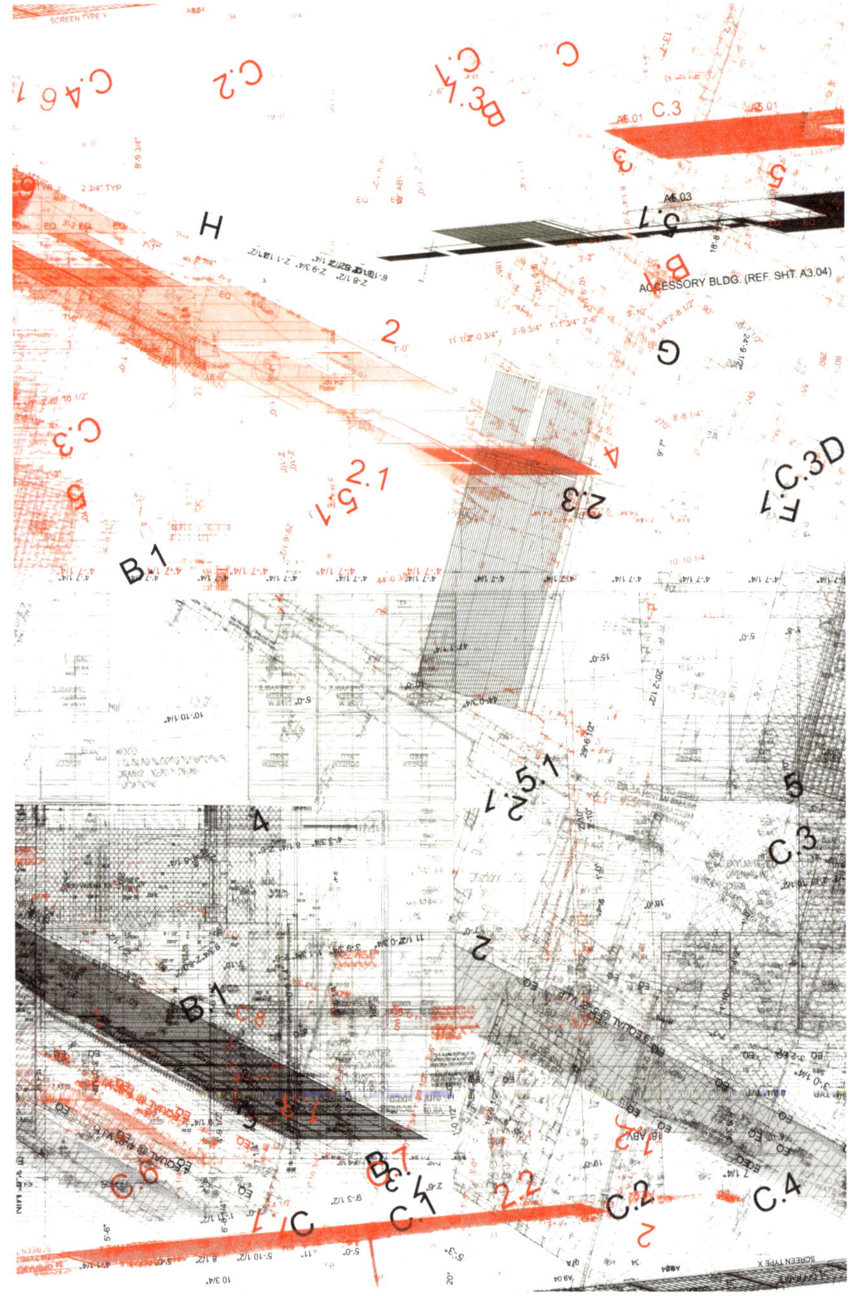

C.8
6.2
C.3
2.3
G
FOLD IN WALL
ACCESSORY BLDG
OVERFLOW DRAIN
SCREEN TYPE X

ACCESSORY BLDG (REF SHT A3.04)
C.3D
C.2
C.4
C.1

ACCESSORY BLDG. (REF. SHT A3.04)

TIMELAPSE

01.19.2010

08.19.2017

PROJECT CREDITS

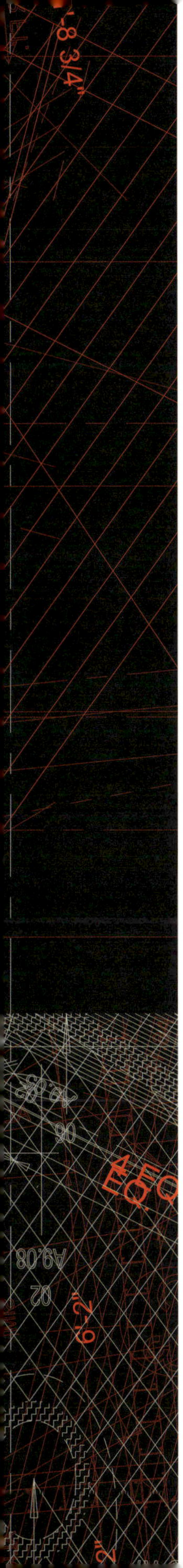

LOCATION:	PACIFIC PALISADES, CALIFORNIA
YEAR:	2018
LOT SIZE:	1.8 ACRES
BUILDING SIZE:	17,500 SQFT
PROJECT TEAM:	
ARCHITECT	SHUBINDONALDSON
PARTNERS-IN-CHARGE	RUSSELL SHUBIN, AIA & ROBIN DONALDSON, AIA
PROJECT ARCHITECT	BRADFORD KELLEY
CONSTRUCTION MANAGER	STONEMARK CONSTRUCTION MANAGEMENT
GENERAL CONTRACTOR	WINTERS-SCHRAM ASSOCIATES
INTERIOR DESIGN	MAGNI KALMAN DESIGN
LANDSCAPING ARCHITECT	AHBE LANDSCAPE ARCHITECTS
STRUCTURAL ENGINEER	JLA
CIVIL ENGINEER	FUSCOE ENGINEERING
MEP CONSULTANT	VISION MECHANICAL SERVICES
LIGHTING CONSULTANT	HLB LIGHTING DESIGN
AUDIOVISUAL CONSULTANT	AUDIO COMMAND SYSTEMS
ART CURATION	MICHAEL THOMAS
ACOUSTICAL ENGINEER	NEWSON BROWN ACOUSTICS
MILLWORK	MILLER WOODWORKING; SPECTRUM OAK, FINISH RITE, MARKSMAN
POOL CONSULTANT	H2O DESIGN

FIRM PROFILE

ShubinDonaldson

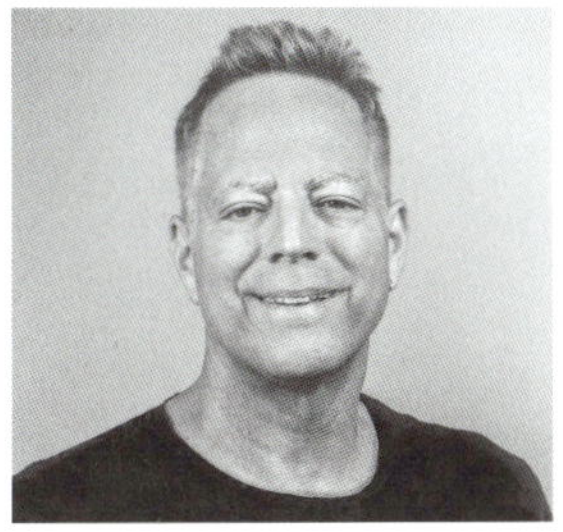

RUSSELL SHUBIN, AIA

Russell Shubin, AIA, is a native Southern Californian, being born and raised in Los Angeles. He received his architecture degree at Cal Poly, San Luis Obispo, studied at the L'Ecole d'Art et d'Architecture in Fontainebleau, and was an Associate at the Blurock Partnership before founding ShubinDonaldson Architects in 1990. Russell is active in the AIA, local development organizations, and regularly speaks on architecture and design panels throughout Los Angeles.

Russell has a passion for distilled ideas, elemental diagrams, and developing strong and relevant narratives that question assumptions about what it means to be current in today's context. His reputation for thoughtful and detailed work stems from a deep investment and intentionality in crafting unique elements and the delineation and articulation of materials. Russell's involvement in the development community has established robust relationships leading to a thriving luxury residential practice serving an international clientele, alongside mixed-use, multi-family, and commercial office projects contributing to the Southern California landscape.

ROBIN DONALDSON, AIA

A fourth-generation Southern Californian, Robin Donaldson, AIA, was born and raised within the SoCal surf and skate culture. Before founding ShubinDonaldson, he received a Bachelor's in Studio Art at UCSB, focusing on painting and printmaking. He then attended the Southern California Institute of Architecture, receiving his Master of Architecture and winning the Henry Adams Medal. During his SCI_Arc studies, Robin began working with Morphosis Architects and served as the Project Architect on the Crawford Residence. In 1990, Donaldson founded ShubinDonaldson Architects. Today he lectures at AIA events, academic institutions, devotes time to AIA advisory boards, and serves on community planning advisory boards across Southern California.

Donaldson's creative force is at the heart of advancing SD's design ethos. He leads the firms' investigations between buildings and topography/landscape integration, representation and drawing sensibilities, and unique fabrication methodologies. His interest in exploring new possibilities for conventional building typologies also includes leading ShubinDonaldson's research and development efforts.

MARK HERSHMAN

A native Southern Californian, Mark Hershman graduated from Woodbury University in 1997. After studying abroad at Sorbonne University in Paris, France, he began his professional career studying with Anthony J. Lumsden, FAIA. Joining ShubinDonaldson in 2000, Mark was integral to the many ShubinDonaldson's early signature projects that helped define the future of "creative" commercial interiors, which has now become the norm. In 2017, he was elevated to Partner, becoming the first to join the Founding Partners to drive the firm's vision forward.

During his 20-year tenure with ShubinDonaldson, Mark has led the firm into new territory, branching into ground-up mixed-use, multi-family projects and advancing the conversation regarding adaptive reuse into more significant campus developments, which are redefining the urban landscape of LA. Mark is continually scouting for new opportunities, questioning new methods of living and working, and technology's role in the discipline. His relentless attention to craft, detail, and the design process has made him a lynchpin at the core of SD's reputation for innovative, award-winning design.

BOOK CREDITS

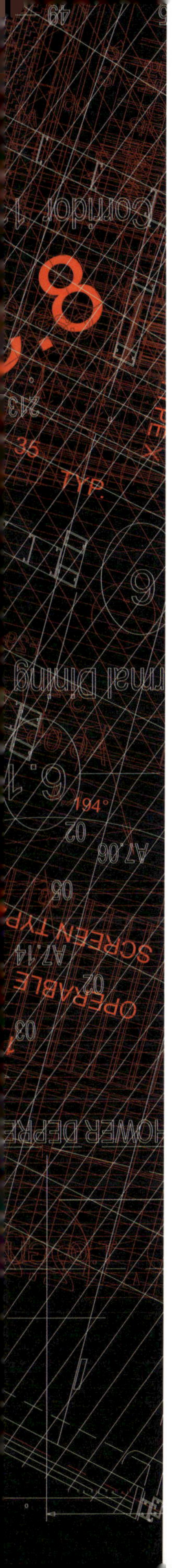

BOOK DESIGN

ART DIRECTION / DESIGN: ROBIN DONALDSON, AIA
EDITOR: F. MYLES SCIOTTO, PH.D.
GRAPHICS COORDINATOR: COLIN RICKARD
SKETCHES: ROBIN DONALDSON, AIA
MODELS: BRADFORD KELLEY
PLANS / SECTIONS: LINGCHEN "SANDY" LIAO
DETAILS: BRADFORD KELLEY
MASKING DRAWINGS: ROBIN DONALDSON, AIA / MIKE NESBIT
COPY EDITS: JULIA VAN DEN HOUT | ORIGINAL COPY

PHOTOGRAPHY

FERNANDO GUERRA: 1-3 / 6-7 / 11-16 / 20-21 / 25-26 / 40-41 / 46-47 / 52-53 / 58-59 / 62-64 / 68
70-83 / 93-95 / 102-103 / 108 / 113 / 116-119 / 123 / 138-139 / 146

ROGER DAVIES: 4-5 / 18-19 / 22-23 / 28-29 / 34-35 / 42-45 / 48-51 / 54-57 / 60 / 65-67 / 69 / 92
100-101 / 106-111 / 122

TAIYO WATANABE: 124-125 / 130-131

ShubinDonaldson

LOS ANGELES OFFICE

3751 Robertson Blvd.
Culver City, CA
T. 310.204.0688

SANTA BARBARA OFFICE

414A Anacapa Street, Ste 101
Santa Barbara, CA
T. 805.682.7000

ORANGE COUNTY OFFICE

32 Executive Park, Ste 115
Irvine, CA
T. 714.352.5353

info@shubindonaldson.com
www.shubindonaldson.com

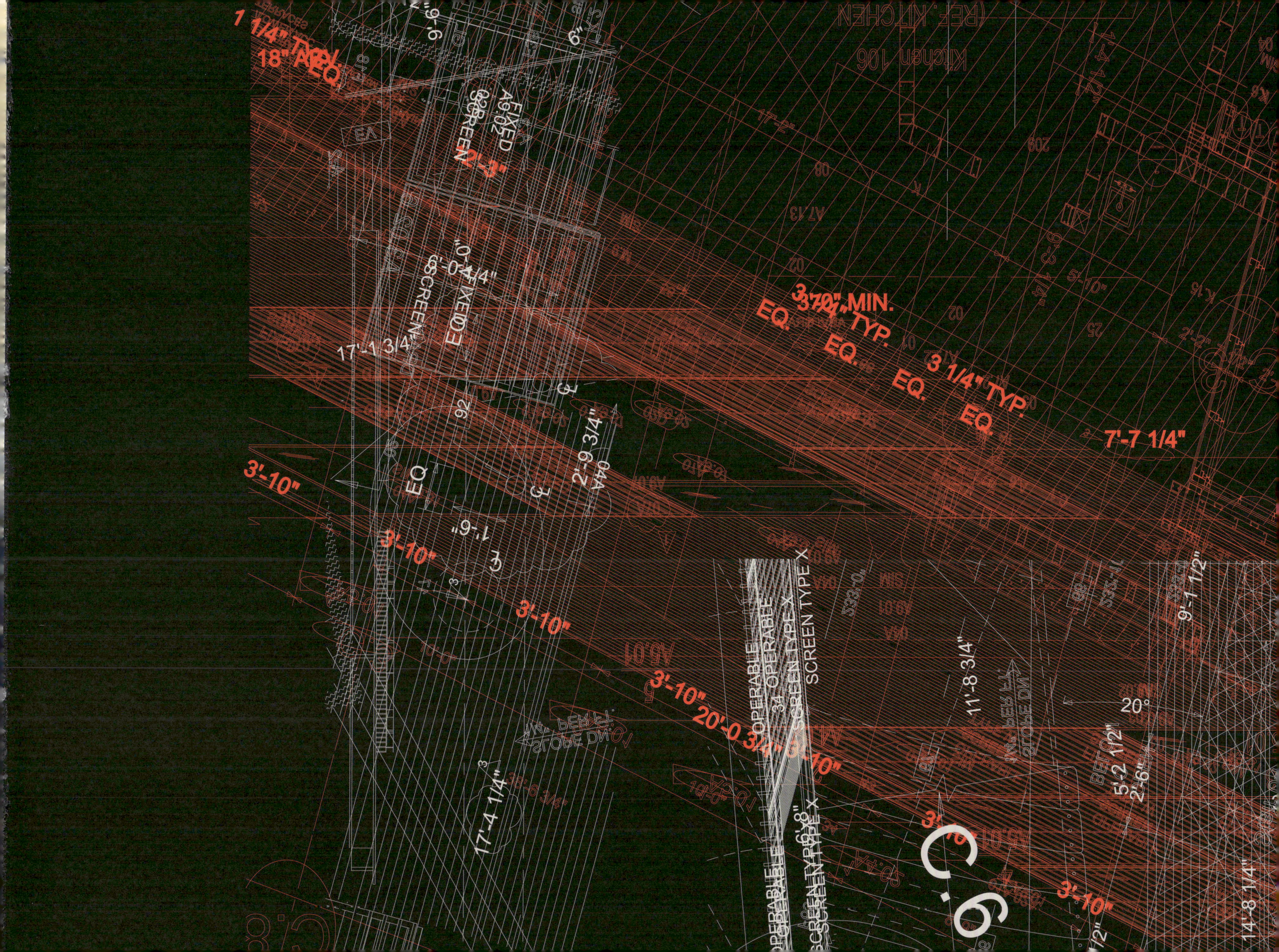

18" REQ.
2'-3"
3'-0" MIN.
3 1/4" TYP.
EQ.
3 1/4" TYP.
7'-7 1/4"
17'-1 3/4"
3'-10"
2'-9 3/4"
20'-0 3/4"
11'-8 3/4"
20°
5'-2 1/2"
17'-4 1/4"
9'-1 1/2"
14'-8 1/4"
SCREEN TYPE X
OPERABLE
C.6